The Shepherd Within

Following God's incarnational initiative to
fullness of life beyond institutional control

Father Anne

Scripture quotations are from the New Revised Standard Version Bible: Catholic Edition, copyright © 1989, 1993 National Council of the Churches of Christ in the United States of America. Used by permission. All rights reserved worldwide.

ISBN 979-8-9931616-0-0 (print)
ISBN 979-8-9931616-1-7 (e-book)
Library of Congress Control Number: 2025921061

Editor: Jill Peterfeso
Editor: Kristen Johnson
Cover: ebooklaunch.com
Artwork: Christ Pantocrator (author unknown)

Published in the United States of America by
Father Anne Ministries
P.O. Box 7054 | Albuquerque, NM 87102
www.fatheranne.com
www.shepherdwithin.com

TABLE OF CONTENTS

"My sheep hear my voice.
I know them, and they follow me."

—John 10:27

PREFACE

After a profound encounter with God at age 29, I started to hear the vocation to be a Roman Catholic priest. The only problem, of course, is that the Roman Catholic Church does not ordain women to the priesthood. This has not stopped God from relentlessly calling me to this path for two decades.

In the early years of my embrace of Catholicism, I could better bear the dissonance between the institution's claims about women and the movement of God's Spirit in my life. While the institution said no, God was forming me as a priest through unofficial avenues. I was mentored by priests, worked closely with priests, and was educated alongside priests. I served in every liturgical ministry, presided over communion services, learned how to lead retreats and preach the Word. Eventually, after I received my seminary degree, I even came to co-pastor a parish as a pastoral administrator, a modern ecclesiological role developed to try to stem the tide of need resulting from the diminishing numbers of male priests. Over the years, I continually found myself adjacent to ordained priestly ministry, my gifts repeatedly affirmed by various communities. While the institutional Church formally excluded me from the ordination track, God's nimble Spirit was navigating around these obstructions to make me the priest that God desired.

Still, I could only go so far. After many years of education, training, and growth within the institutional Church, I finally hit the stained-glass ceiling: I had learned all I could through unofficial channels and now the Church was preventing me from fully blossoming into a priest. I could go no further: I could not receive the sacrament of holy orders in the Roman Catholic Church.

What was I to do? I was plunged into darkness. I felt God's desires so strongly they would keep me awake at night. God haunted me—haunts me still—every moment of every day, "You are my priest." I counter back, sometimes angrily, sometimes desperately, always faithfully, "Yes I know, Lord, but they will not let me serve you this way." God's

Spirit flares in response, "Make them listen." "How? What can I do?" Over all these years, God's answer has remained the same: "Follow me."

Since those days I have grown in my theological understanding of the incarnation. Christianity speaks of Jesus as the incarnation of God, and generally the focus is almost entirely on how Jesus reveals God. Yes, indeed, Jesus makes visible the heart and nature and desires of God, but equally important, he reveals humanity—that is, how God envisions the relationship between God and humanity to unfold. Jesus makes known what a human life rightly and fully aligned with God looks like, what is possible when human beings consent to and cooperate with how God desires to enter historical time through them. Jesus, by virtue of his humanity, reveals that every human is invited to become an incarnational pathway of God's self-expression into the world. Through the power of the Holy Spirit, all of us have the great honor of putting flesh on the living God, becoming a source of God's inbreaking into the world. This is the incarnational principle that underlies the whole of life.

Contemplating my experiences through the lens of this incarnational design of life, I have learned over the years that my call to priesthood is not simply about what God is asking me to do _for_ God. In a more surface way, yes, this is true: I do the actions of priestly ministries for God. But the far deeper spiritual reality is that my call to priesthood is fundamentally about how God wants to express God's self through me, how God is initiating a particular incarnational pathway through me and into the world to bless it with goodness. God has given me—indeed, all of us—a unique share in God's life to uplift those in our little corner of creation. In other words, priesthood is the primary pathway that God desires to travel in and through me into the world to touch others.

We all have these incarnational pathways—such as, parent or teacher or inventor or poet or peacemaker or comedian or community organizer—the possibilities of God's self-expression in us are endless. This is the Shepherd Within: our particular share in the life of God that is to unfold through us to make life good. We bless others with our blessing, and by blessing others we are blessed. This holy exchange among God's people not only gives our personal lives meaning and fulfillment, but the goodness is so good that it serves as a beacon of light to attract others to God, so that they, too, can discover God and be brought by the Holy Spirit into loving relationship. We all have our share in making real God's dream of a world that works for all.

In addition to blessing others with goodness, these incarnational pathways of our lives provide the ongoing, ever-present opportunity to experience God's presence, to be drawn into heartfelt oneness with the living God. As our spiritual senses sharpen, we enter a different spiritual dimension. Daily life becomes so rich and profound that what once appeared ordinary is transfigured into the extraordinary. There is no more fulfilling experience available to human beings than communion with God—not only for us, but for God also, who loves us into being to share life together as intimate companions in love.

In my case, however, the Roman Catholic Church is interfering in God's desires for my life in God. As a result of this institutional obstruction, I suffer—or more accurately, God suffers within me, and I experience God's suffering as my own. I sense the ongoing struggle of God's frustrated Spirit, which longs to break free and flow, but cannot because of the institutional Church's obstruction. By the word "frustration," I do not strictly mean agitation, but an incarnational pressure that continues to build, like rushing water against a dam. The pressure increases as the Spirit relentlessly seeks to find ways to overcome the obstruction and enter the world as God intends.

On the one hand, my life is greatly advantaged. I have the white privilege that intersects with and is amplified by American privilege. I have access to fresh and healthy food, clean water, and safe shelter. I received a good public education and went on to earn advanced degrees from excellent universities. I have access to doctors and dentists. I own a car that runs and I can afford to put gas in it. I do not live in constant fear of police brutality or bombs being dropped on my home (though the rapid descent into authoritarianism in the U.S. is deeply troubling). Even with all the sexism that women in America have to endure, I live an immensely fortunate life in a world plagued by unspeakable violence, crushing poverty and exploitation, and cruel oppression.

While it is true my life is greatly advantaged, it is also true that I live a haunted life. Bearing the incarnational pressure of God's desires for priesthood is all consuming. "[W]ithin me there is something like a burning fire shut up in my bones; I am weary with holding it in, and I cannot" (Jeremiah 20:9). Frequently I feel as if I will quite literally burst into the flames of God's desires. At other times I want to go to sleep and never wake up. I am imprisoned, trapped between the unstoppable God and the immovable Roman Catholic Church. Day and night I feel it: there is no escape. Sometimes I think I will be crushed to death by the might of these two forces converging upon me.

Add to this haunting the torment of witnessing men of all stripes afforded the opportunity to live out their priesthood while my own priestly gifts languish simply because I am a woman, and the grief of enduring excommunication—a punishment so severe that not even the male priests sick with pedophilia, nor the bishops who hid them, receive it: it's all a bitter pill to swallow, especially for someone with a heart so fiercely devoted to God and to the wellbeing of the institutional Church itself. If I am not careful, I will end up hard-hearted and brimming with resentment, even amidst a life of significant privilege. I must make the conscious decision each day to live focused on the fullness of life that God pours out upon me, even as I am condemned to a path of death by the Church that is supposed to be my home. Some days I am better at this practice of joy than others. I still have much room to grow in the spiritual life.

Whatever the difficulties, however, I would not trade my peculiar and surprising path—its exquisite torture, its secret exhilaration. I would not trade being haunted by God's dreams of what could be for this world if human beings would just cooperate. I would not trade the pleasure of God's whispers of gratitude into my heart for fidelity to the path. I would not trade the burden of God's anguish at the suffering that humans inflict upon ourselves and on creation. Life is worth living, even as I forever mourn what might have been, if only the Roman Catholic Church would listen.

Of course, I must admit that none of this has been my choice. Lazarus did not ask to be raised, after all. If you inquired twenty years ago where I would be on this day, never in a million years would I have guessed it would be here: a Roman Catholic priest illegally ordained in 2021; unjustly excommunicated as a criminal; humbly living on the handouts of generous people who know that what the Catholic Church is doing to women is wrong. I did not choose this path, but I did choose to fully give myself over to God's invitation. With my yes to God, I have been swept up onto a journey that is not my own, and I would not trade it. Not for a moment.

So, my life now is about righting this wrong for God, for God's people, for creation. The exclusion of women from priesthood impacts all people everywhere because the Roman Catholic Church is an institution like no other. It spans *every country*; it is the largest nongovernmental provider of healthcare and education in the world; it is a religious entity with statehood (Vatican City); it has observer status at the United Nations where it lobbies on issues that affect women and girls around the world, whether they are Catholic or not; it has formal diplomatic relations with foreign countries; it is one of the largest landowners in the world. As you can see, the Roman Church is an odd global empire, unique unto itself.

Yet, even with its bottomless resources and scores of brilliant theologians, the Roman Catholic Church is still teaching and upholding the original sin—that women are somehow inferior by nature, designed by God to be a second order of creation destined for subjugation by men. This is a deceitful theory of the human person, shared and propagated across culture, country, and religion, and its profound error is evidenced by its bitter fruit: domination, war, poverty, exploitation, dehumanization and violence of every kind. God never at any point has intended for life to be organized into patriarchy. Yet, the Roman Catholic Church still perpetuates this ungodly myth, and with its global sprawl and access to levers of power, it delivers a devastating blow to God's dream of salvation on earth. Bringing this one doctrine into alignment with God— welcoming the full participation of women at every level of Church life—will unleash a flood of goodness so profound that it will uplift the entire world, especially in those places where the lives of women are truly desperate. How many issues can you name where one source of authority affects *billions* of people?

This is my cross. What is yours? All of us suffer at the hands of powerful institutions that in subtle and ruthless ways obstruct how God desires to incarnate in and through us. In answer to this challenge, I offer you this book, which flows from my experience of God over these last twenty-plus years. This text is a collection of insights about the spiritual principles that govern life on earth—laws that emerge from what I call God's incarnational initiative. I explore how we can recognize God's inbreaking into our lives, the ways institutions seek to obstruct this inbreaking, and how we can overcome these obstructions to become who we are to bless the world with goodness. My hope is that through deep engagement with this content, you are better able to recognize the Shepherd Within, so that above all you can grow in heartfelt communion with the living God, who wants nothing more than to lead you to a life of joy and fulfillment that uplifts the world—institutional obstruction be damned.

In prayer,
Father Anne +

a note to readers

This book is designed to facilitate encounter with the living God. In a certain sense, it is laid out as a retreat in everyday life in that the text will lead you from movement to movement. The first three parts explore the hidden spiritual principles that govern life on earth. With this foundation in place, the final section offers spiritual exercises that guide you in a discovery of how these governing spiritual principles are at work in your own life. The best way to approach engagement with this book is to see the first three parts as preparation for Part Four. In this way, the spiritual exercises are not an afterthought to place in an appendix, but the central purpose of the text: they help you carve out time for an experience of God that gives you insight into who you are for God and for the world.

May this book bring you closer to God.

+

**PART ONE:
THE INCARNATION**

"Some things have to be believed to be seen."

—Ralph Hogdson

Engaging with Part One

Part One explores the hidden spiritual realities of the incarnation faithfully at work in our lives. Chapter 1 explains the concept of God's incarnational initiative. Chapter 2 points to specific areas of our lives where we can recognize God's presence incarnating within and through us. Chapter 3 describes the fruit of honoring God's incarnational desires. These chapters bring into focus what is possible when we recognize, consent to, and cooperate with the incarnational principle that governs life.

1 | UNDERSTAND

Tina Crawford's world was shattered in 2014 when her only son, Ira Hopkins, was killed during a robbery on his 35th birthday. Though rage and the desire for vengeance flooded her at first, in the months between Ira's murder and the conclusion of the courtroom proceedings, Tina was somehow moved to forgiveness. Discovering an unexpected tie to one of the defendants, 18-year-old Jy'Aire Smith-Pennick, Tina began exchanging letters and phone calls with him and learned his story. Jy'Aire was homeless during his youth for large stretches of time, bouncing from place to place. He then endured a series of staggering losses: at 14 his mother died, at 17 his father, and at 18 his stepmother. He started selling heroin to survive and was persuaded into robbing a stranger: Ira Hopkins. In learning his story, Tina was moved from forgiveness to mercy.

As Jy'Aire endured the years in prison, Tina motivated him to pursue his education. He earned a high school diploma, an associate degree, and became a certified peer specialist to help other inmates. In October 2024, Tina spoke on Jy'Aire's behalf to the Delaware Board of Pardons. She reflected on her experience, sharing that she lost a son, but gained another through the process. Deeply moved, the Board unanimously voted to commute Jy'Aire's sentence. Once released, Tina and Jy'Aire founded the IRA Foundation, a nonprofit whose mission is to help at-risk youth by teaching skills like carpentry, bricklaying, music, and photography. "[T]he one who was seated on the throne said, 'See, I am making all things new'" (Revelation 21:5).

The relationship between Tina and Jy'Aire is a striking example of the fullness of life that is possible when we embrace the spiritual laws that govern our life together on earth. While there are physical principles embedded within the material world, there are also—equally important—spiritual principles built into the design of life. Like physical laws, these spiritual laws operate whether or not we acknowledge them. If we ignore these hidden spiritual realities, we create great pain and suffering for life on earth, but if we become aware of and honor them, then we make real the goodness that God intends for us in the present moment. This book is an exploration of these hidden governing spiritual principles, understood through the lens of the incarnation.

God enters into history

God longs to be known—truly known—by us. The whole of biblical scripture captures this core desire of God, who over and over enters historical circumstances through inspired figures and saving acts that comfort, guide, liberate, and challenge the people to a life of love in God. As the prophet Hosea proclaims, "For I desire steadfast love and not sacrifice, the knowledge of God rather than burnt offerings" (Hosea 6:6). Though God continues down through the ages to explain and demonstrate to the people who God is and what God envisions for life together, they struggle, just as we do, to understand. God never gives up, however, faithfully communicating God's love and desires until

God finally enters time in the fullest material revelation possible: Jesus. In Jesus, God makes visible God's dream for salvation—that is, the goodness that is God's very self, inbreaking into the present moment to bring about fullness of life for all creation.

When we consider the life of Jesus within the arc of salvation history in the scriptures, we see that God is trying to communicate with increasing clarity what the inbreaking of God's presence looks and feels like—the unmistakable pattern of outcomes and sensibilities that unfold from a direct encounter with the living God. Jesus crystallizes and makes visible these hidden realities so that humanity can better recognize them: God is Mercy that heals the sick and restores them to community (Mark 5:25-34); God is Teaching that inspires compassion, hope, and generosity of heart (Matthew 18:21-22); God is Challenge that disrupts systems of power (Matthew 23:1-29); God is Hope that brings good news to the poor (Matthew 11:4-5). While God will always remain Mystery ultimately beyond our grasp, at the same time God makes God's self intelligible to us in the life of Jesus.

Because Jesus is the incarnation of God, his ministry is not simply actions done for God, in the name of God, or even by God. Rather, *they are God*. God enters into a particular moment and context within history to bring about God's desired intentions of goodness in that moment. In other words, God does not give us an object called freedom: God enters *as* freedom. God does not give us an object called healing: God enters *as* healing. God does not give us an object called reconciliation, God enters *as* reconciliation. God always gives us God— that particular share of God's self that is needed for goodness to become real in that particular time and place.

God's essential drive to incarnate

God's drive to incarnate into historical reality is a deeply essential aspect of God's nature. At God's core is this creative desire for self-expression in the material world, to incarnate into perceivable materiality. Put more simply, God incarnates fully in Jesus, but not only in Jesus. Through the power of the Holy Spirit, God expresses something of God's self in all creation—the land, its creatures, the water. "The spirit of the Lord has filled the world"

(Wisdom 1:7), and thus, in God "we live and move and have our being" (Acts 17:28). God mysteriously exists beyond time but is also deeply embedded within it, animating all creation. This drive to express God's self in materiality—God's incarnational initiative— underpins the whole of life on earth.

Because God's Spirit is pulsing throughout creation, all life offers the opportunity for encounter with the living God. The creature knows the Creator: our bodies are given the spiritual senses to inherently recognize the One who loved us into being. As Jesus explains, "My sheep hear my voice. I know them, and they follow me" (John 10:27). Our task is to sharpen these senses so that we can grow aware of God's ongoing revelatory presence in and around us. With practice we can become increasingly cognizant of God, who then, through the power of the Holy Spirit, pours out into us something of God's very self. The more we encounter the living God, the more we come to intimately know God and the more we come to know ourselves. Through this ongoing encounter with God we are transformed, and everyday life overflows with meaning.

Too often, however, we live altogether unaware of God's inbreaking presence within us and around us. This oblivion can lead to a shallow relationship with creation where we regard it as a collection of objects for use and abuse rather than as the inbreaking of the living God. This shallow seeing produces a throwaway culture that views relationships as transactional—a way of seeing that foments greed, cruelty, and the exploitation not just of natural resources and animals, but of humanity itself. An unconsciousness to God's presence in creation sees laborers in factories and fields as expendable machines; permits experimentation on Black people without their consent; forces Indigenous peoples onto reservations; imprisons women and girls in sexual slavery; over-fishes the seas and over-mines the land; poisons the air and water. "The earth lies polluted under its inhabitants; for they have transgressed laws, violated the statutes, broken the everlasting covenant. Therefore a curse devours the earth" (Isaiah 24:5-6). Without right seeing there is no reverence, only a barren utility. When we awaken to God's incarnating presence in and around us, the veil falls from our eyes: every bush burns with the presence of God

(Exodus 3:1-3), every eye glimmers with its share of God's Holy Spirit (1 Corinthians 3:16). Life is transformed and we become moved to live with gentleness, humility, and awe.

Humanity as a pathway of the incarnation

While Jesus reveals God's nature and God's core drive for self-expression, he also reveals humanity—that is, how God imagines the relationship between God and humanity to unfold. The life and ministry of Jesus makes visible what is possible when a human being is in alignment with God's desires for that person's life. The relationship between God and Jesus is one of mutual self-gift: God freely and fully pours forth God's self into Jesus; Jesus receives all that God offers, then freely and fully returns it back to God in service of God's project of salvation. This mutual outpouring of the self creates a communion of love through the power of the Holy Spirit, bringing about the good that God intends.

This trinitarian love is how God imagines spending life with each one of us. The capacity for this deep and profound intimacy with God is built into our natural design as humans. We are invited to participate in the life of God: to fully and freely receive the share of God's self that God wants to give us, and then to direct it fully and freely back to God to create the world of goodness that God intends for all creation. When we say yes to God and bring our lives into alignment with what God is initiating, we become a powerful incarnational pathway of God's inbreaking into everyday life.

We see this dynamic profoundly at work in the life of Scott Harrison. For ten years Scott lived as a wildly successful club promoter in Manhattan. He enjoyed VIP status and life with celebrities, yet he eventually came to feel that his life was empty and devoid of meaning. After some significant soul-searching, he decided to leave nightlife to embark on a year of service. Rejected by dozens of humanitarian organizations because of his unusual background, he refused to give up. Finally he was accepted as a photojournalist by Mercy Ships floating hospitals. Scott was taken to Liberia, where he spent several months documenting patients' stories and witnessing extreme poverty, which included the devastating effects of dirty water. Transformed by his encounter with the poor, Scott returned to Manhattan and launched a non-profit organization called *charity: water* with a mission to bring clean and safe water to all people everywhere. Twenty years later, he and his remarkable team have completed 186,000 projects across 29 countries, bringing clean water to more than 20 million people.

Scott's inspiring story is a striking example of what is possible when a human life comes into alignment with what God desires to do for the world through and with us. "I am the vine, you are the branches. Those who abide in me and I in them bear much fruit" (John 15:5). God initiates the path, and we, in turn, consent to and give ourselves over to it, and abundance flows. We can never know where the path will ultimately take us, nor what is truly possible through our companionship with the living God. The only way to unearth this alternate future is to faithfully continue to follow where God's Holy Spirit leads.

Each of us has been given this sacred invitation to discover how God desires to incarnate through us to bless the world. As we grow in awareness of God's communications, we can more fully receive our share in the life of God and more fully offer it back to God in service of making real God's dream of salvation on earth. God is the end and the beginning—the source from which our life proceeds, the end to which we direct this gift of life. When we give ourselves over to God's incarnational initiative, life swells with meaning and we can never return to the way of unseeing.

However, when we fail to recognize the incarnational design of life, we can be plagued by dissatisfaction, agitation, and emptiness. This discontent is counter to our nature and often drives us to pursue meaning and fulfillment in the pleasures and distractions of the world. While such things may provide a passing contentment, they will never truly fulfill. In fact, they cannot: at its most fundamental level, human life is designed for conscious, intimate companionship with God. The psalmist captures this longing so beautifully: "As a deer longs for flowing streams, so my soul longs for you, O God. My soul thirsts for God, for the living God. When shall I come and behold the face of God" (Psalm 42:1-2). When relationship with God is missing, we lack a true understanding of who we are and what our lives are for, and we become restless at the level of self.

Importantly, intimate communion with God does not mean we will not make mistakes or cause harm to ourselves or others. We are not, and never will be, perfect. Indeed, God does not expect perfection, but asks for fidelity: fidelity to the incarnational principle—to God's promise to enter history and overcome our mistakes and wounds. The more we participate in the life of God, the more we can readily receive the outpouring of God's self into our being. This ongoing encounter heals, teaches, reconciles, prunes— all which lead us to fulfillment and right-living. This neverending education by the Spirit continues over the arc of our entire lives. As long as we keep offering God access to our being, God will continue to pour out the Spirit of renewal into our lives and bring us to new life (2 Corinthians 5:17). This is God's promise; it is a promise we can trust.

As we grow in familiarity and continue to bring ourselves into greater alignment with God, we become a living sign of the goodness of God. God shines through us more and more brightly, reaching into time not just to uplift us, but also to attract others to God. "You are the light of the world…Let your light shine before others, so that they may see your good works and give glory to your Father in heaven" (Matthew 5:14-16). Maybe we have experienced being drawn to God through another person—perhaps through our grandmother's particular way of praying the rosary, or in listening to our teacher tell the story of Rosa Parks, or in seeing the joyous smile of Bishop Desmond Tutu. When the light of God shines forth in God's people, the Holy Spirit uses it to enkindle the hearts of those who witness it, inviting them into their own mystical encounter with the living God.

***

What is your share in the life of God? What goodness is made real in the world through your life in God? It is a great mystery why God has designed life in this way, with us as companions in the co-creation of a life of goodness together. As the life of Jesus reveals, the more we give ourselves over to God's incarnational initiative, the more fully God can enter into every time and place to bring about the fullness of life that God intends. Through our fidelity to this path, we become an incarnational people, a tide rising across creation as the shining content of God's dream of mercy, justice, and salvation for all.

+

2 | IDENTIFY

When we watch Simone Biles do a floor routine or witness Amanda Gorman proclaim spoken word, we are encountering the inbreaking of God's presence into a specific time and place. They each have a particular share in the life of God that is being made real for us to appreciate and enjoy: God as creativity, God as precision, God as strength, God as challenge, God as brilliance. While it might be easier to see God's incarnational initiative at work in others, we too are each a unique path of God's self-gift into the world. We can begin to develop our awareness of the Shepherd Within by contemplating some essential aspects of our lives.

Vocation as the deepest orientation toward God

When Milo Runkle was fifteen, he was profoundly impacted by a local animal abuse case. A teacher of a high school agricultural class brought in piglets from his pig farm for a dissection project. Somehow one of the piglets was still alive. A student who worked part-time on the farm for the teacher took the piglet by the hind legs and slammed its skull into the ground to kill it. Though this was standard agricultural practice, the school community was scandalized and animal cruelty cases were brought against both the teacher and the student helper. However, the farming community immediately rallied around the teacher and student, and the cases were promptly dismissed. In that moment, Milo experienced his vocation: farmed animals had no one to advocate for them. The nonprofit Mercy for Animals was born.

Milo and a small group of volunteers began putting themselves at great risk of imprisonment by sneaking onto factory farms to document the gruesome cruelty as well as to rescue sick and injured animals. Twenty-five years later, Mercy for Animals is a global leader in the struggle to end industrial animal agriculture. They expose and fight the hidden brutality on factory farms, which includes the practice of ripping off the testicles of male piglets without anesthetic; the extreme confinement of pigs—animals smarter than dogs and human toddlers—in crates so small they can only stand or lay down; the cramming of egg-laying chickens into torturous battery cages with little room to move; the killing of hundreds of millions of male chicks each year on egg farms by gassing them to death or putting them fully conscious into high speed grinders; the pumping of so many steroids into broiler chickens that they become deformed and unable to stand due to the increased size of their breasts; the ruthless perpetual impregnation of dairy cows, who cry out in grief each time their terrified calves are ripped away from them moments after birth so humans can seize the milk intended for their young. These animals—who have a share in the life of God—never get to experience fresh air or even walk, only to end up in the trash when Americans waste approximately 40% of the U.S. food supply each year. It is an appalling disregard for God and for God's sacred creation. "How long will the land mourn, and the grass of every field wither? For the wickedness of those who live in it the animals and the birds are swept away" (Jeremiah 12:4).

These sentient creatures suffer unspeakable brutality precisely so that agribusiness corporations can rake in billions of dollars in profits at their expense. Milo has inspired a movement of people through education, policy work, and undercover investigations to stand up to some of the most powerful corporate interests in the world in defense of a truly voiceless and exploited group. "You did not choose me but I chose you. And I appointed you to go and bear fruit, fruit that will last" (John 15:16). Through their unflagging devotion, Mercy for Animals impacts the welfare of hundreds of millions of animals annually—bearing much fruit, fruit that will last.

What is your vocation? What is your life for and for whom? Vocation is often understood as the primary way to serve God. While this is a reasonable definition, vocation is far more richly recognized as a principal path that God desires to take through us and with us into the world to bless it with goodness. Rather than a set of tasks we do for God, or even a way of life, vocation is a powerful pathway of God's inbreaking.

Vocation is experienced at the deepest level of self. God implants God's own desire for our lives into the depths of our heart, and we feel God's desire as our own. In this sense, vocation is a point of unity between Creator and creature, a touchpoint of convergence where two become one—a unique communion of lives made possible by the power of the Holy Spirit. As we live out our vocation, God enters through us to bring about the goodness that God intends in our little corner of the world.

While vocation can overlap with employment, this is not necessarily the case. A true understanding of vocation goes beyond career paths to recognize it as core to who we are in God—as a creature called to a share in God's project of goodness for all creation. "For we are what he has made us, created in Christ Jesus for good works, which God prepared beforehand to be our way of life" (Ephesians 2:10). Maybe we have a vocation to be a teacher or inventor or farmer or lawyer or detective, or to accompany people who are dying, or to beautify spaces to give people comfort and inspiration. Maybe we have a vocation to parenthood, or to organize our neighbors to resist corporate polluters, or to create a network of gardens that nourish a community trapped in a food desert. For Angelita Castro Kelly it was a career in aerospace, leading her to become the first female Mission Operations Manager of NASA. For Quaker Isaac Hopper it was to organize part of the Underground Railroad to help Black people trapped in slavery find freedom. Whether a vocation is recognized as a paid position of employment is not an indication of its validity or value in God's project of goodness on earth. Many vocations are jobs and many exist outside of formal employment structures: all are essential to making God's dream of salvation on earth a reality.

It is possible, even likely, to have multiple vocations at one time or to experience different vocations over the arc of our lives. For example, maybe we experience a vocation to be a teacher, and also a parent and spouse. Maybe we feel the call to be a priest or vowed religious and also have a call within a call to serve a particular marginalized community, like Sr. Helen Prejean, who advocates for and counsels those condemned by society to death row. Maybe early in life we had a vocation to be on Broadway, but in later years feel moved to teach students who have little to no access to the arts. Vocations are the deep commitments that orient us for significant phases of time to our share of God's project of flourishing.

While vocation is the holy invitation to cooperate with God's incarnational initiative at the deepest level of self, it is important not to romanticize this notion. At times vocation can ruthlessly and unexpectedly descend upon us, as in the case of parents whose children were killed in the mass shooting at Sandy Hook Elementary School and who now feel the vocation of working for gun reform in the United States; or as in the case of Oskar Schindler, who experienced a slow, but deep conversion from being a member of the Nazi party to using his business to shield Jews from the ruthless Nazi regime. While vocation provides our lives with profound meaning, it is also true that vocation can be an arduous cross to bear. When we say yes to our vocations, we are swept up onto a journey that is not of our own making, one often of great sacrifice.

Vocation is deeply personal, but it is also wholly communal. Because vocation is a primary pathway of God's self-gift, it is not given for our benefit alone, but also for the benefit of the world. A true vocation from God always orients us to the flourishing of others. In this way, each of us is given by God as a gift to others, to bless life with the particular share of God's life that we have been invited by God to give. Through the exchange of gifts among God's people, the Holy Spirit knits us into a communion of goodness on earth.

Gifts and talents as God's self-expression

We can also experience God's incarnational inbreaking in our innate gifts and talents. Maybe we have the ability to sing or cook or write. Maybe we have a remarkable memory, are adept at numbers or with plants, or are skilled at building things. Maybe we are blessed with a childlike innocence, with a dry sense of humor that leaves the room in stitches, or with the bravery that runs into danger instead of away from it.

Our innate gifts and talents are not simply objects we possess. They are God's creative self-expression in us and through us—bestowed on us to give life color and meaning and goodness. Like vocation, our gifts and talents are points of unity between Creator and creature, touchpoints of convergence where two become one through the power of the Holy Spirit. If we approach our inherent gifts and talents as incarnational, we can explore and cultivate them as part of a conscious and vibrant relationship with God: each time we use our gifts, we approach it as an opportunity to grow in awareness of God and grow in intimacy.

Mysteriously, God gives us the freedom to direct our gifts and talents in whatever way we choose. We are free to squander them or even to direct them in ungodly ways for ungodly ends. We see this dynamic epitomized in Harvey Weinstein and Bill Cosby, who used their talents and position to sexually assault women. We see it in Bernie Madoff, who used his genius, grit, and charm to steal billions of dollars from clients. We see it in social media influencers who use their intellect and wit to manipulate information—even to the point of blatantly lying—to advance a particular product from which they financially gain. "Be appalled, O heavens, at this, be shocked, be utterly desolate, says the Lord, for my people have committed two evils: they have forsaken me, the fountain of living water, and dug out cisterns for themselves, cracked cisterns that can hold no water" (Jeremiah 2:12-13). In such cases of deep disorder, people remove God from the center of their lives and place there a substitute, like power, money, or fame. This artificial center simply cannot produce true goodness because that place is only for God, making all else cracked cisterns that can hold no water.

Such twisting of gifts is a fundamental betrayal of God because this dark behavior uses God's own creative self-expression in opposition to God's vision of wellbeing for all creation. As with vocation, our innate gifts and talents are given for the benefit of others as much as they are given for our own satisfaction and joy. "There are varieties of gifts, but the same Spirit; and there are varieties of services, but the same Lord; and there are varieties of activities, but it is the same God who activates all of them in everyone. To each is given the manifestation of the Spirit *for the common good*" (1 Corinthians 12:4-6, emphasis added). Because our gifts are given for the goodness of all, it is our moral obligation to properly order them to be in alignment with what God intends. When we ignore the incarnational design of life to serve the self alone, not only do we hurt others, we also cloud our own being and lose something fundamental to who we are by cutting ourselves off from the deepest fulfillment that can only flow from life in God.

Relational inbreaking of God into everyday life

One day in August 2025, Gary Thynes took his dog to the park. An unfamiliar pit bull approached and started to behave in such a way that indicated a plea for help. Something within Gary strongly moved him to follow the dog, who led him to a tent encampment where two people were unresponsive. Gary called for help, and the couple was rushed to the hospital to receive lifesaving treatment. Gary fostered their dog while they recovered. "Every generous act of giving, with every perfect gift, is from above, coming down from the Father of lights" (James 1:17). Gary gave generously of himself to God in that moment, making himself available to the Spirit for God's saving work at a time of urgent need.

Gary's experience captures the spontaneous, relational inbreaking of God into
everyday life. We have all had this experience:
the deep prompting of God's Holy Spirit to
respond in the moment to a situation or
person that comes before us. These
movements are so powerful that we feel them
viscerally, yet we often dismiss them as
simple instinct or coincidence. Why do we
feel a need to domesticate such experiences?
If we are to take the life and ministry of Jesus
seriously, then we know that God enters into
a specific historical context at specific times
to respond to specific needs: in story after
story in the Gospels, Jesus looks deeply into
the eyes of those who come before him and
offers them spontaneous help (Matthew
14:19-21; John 9:6-7; Mark 2:11-12).

As we grow in the spiritual life and become progressively attuned to the Holy
Spirit's movements within us, we feel these
interior promptings with increasing
frequency. Maybe we are moved by God to
speak a word of consolation to a grieving
coworker, or to offer a meal to someone who
feels lonely and has no home, or to offer help
to someone stranded on the roadside (Luke
10:25-37). God's Spirit ceaselessly roams the

earth, searching for every opportunity to enter time and uplift us. When we cooperate with these spontaneous promptings of the Holy Spirit, we cooperate with God's incarnational initiative to bring about the goodness that God intends in the current circumstances.

God also incarnates as the intimacy between hearts. Recall an experience of enjoying coffee or a walk with a close friend, of spending a night of passion with a true love, of being built up by an encouraging talk from a loving parent. We have all experienced these moments of deep relationality— experiences that are only possible because those involved are fully oriented toward the other, completely present and without pretense.

Such incarnational connection often flows from the act of forgiveness. In 2006, after a 24-hour shift, 20-year-old firefighter Matt Swatzell headed home. Exhausted, he fell asleep at the wheel, killing June Fitzgerald and her unborn baby, and injuring her 19-month-old daughter. June's husband Erik Fitzgerald was a pastor, and with the support of his community, he quickly came to forgive Matt. When the two-year investigation period concluded, the two men met in person. As Matt burst into tears upon seeing Erik, Erik offered him sincere forgiveness. Deeply moved, Matt was overcome with relief, freed from the weight of his mistake (Psalm 32:5). Erik actively pursued a friendship with Matt, helping him move through the enormity of guilt. The two men built a lasting friendship that blossomed and sustained over many years. Forgiveness, whether or not it leads to an ongoing relationship, is one of the most profound experiences of God's inbreaking into time that we can experience. Through the act of forgiveness, God reconciles the world to God's heart.

Intimacy like the deep and pure connection shared between Eirk and Matt is the inbreaking of God into time. When we deeply listen and receive another without judgment, when we give of ourselves honestly and authentically, when we set aside personal agendas to be fully present to another, a mystical communion mysteriously springs forth by the power of the Holy Spirit. Intimacy is not something that God does. Rather, intimacy *is* God; it is God entering the everyday to give life meaning and make life good.

Another pathway of God's relational inbreaking is through self-sacrifice for others. On April 14, 2004, Corporal Jason L. Dunham's squad was conducting a reconnaissance mission during the Iraq War when they encountered an ambush. When an Iraqi soldier released a live grenade, without hesitation Cpl. Dunham shouted a warning and threw himself onto the grenade to shield his fellow Marines. He saved the lives of at least two marines. However, his act of selflessness cost him his life: Jason died eight days later at Bethesda Naval Hospital. "No one has greater love than this, to lay down one's life for one's friends" (John 15:13).

The life of Jesus reveals the absolute centrality of self-sacrifice in making real God's vision of salvation in the present moment. The suffering of sacrifice shows up in infinite ways, as in the perseverance of those who work dehumanizing jobs day after day, month after month, year after year, to provide for their families. It shows up in the willingness to take on the crushing task of laboring for racial justice in America. It shows up in the endless nights of crawling out of bed to breastfeed one's babies. It shows up in the daily commitment of caring for a declining spouse, a parent with

Alzheimer's, or a child with disabilities. At the most fundamental level of existence, God has designed human life not only to be *with* others, but *for* others. Life works the way God intends when we all sacrifice for one another.

***

The daily work of vocation, the cultivation of our innate gifts and talents, the deep connection we experience with others—these are some of the many ways that God's incarnational initiative is at work in our lives. God has designed life so that every moment offers us the opportunity to be drawn into conscious encounter with the living God. As we grow in awareness of and give ourselves over to God's desires for life together, the more vibrant life becomes: rich with the meaning and purpose that can only flow from participating in the life of God. How is your experience of daily life transformed when you become aware of God's inbreaking through you to bless the world with goodness?

+

3 | HONOR

Everything is at stake in honoring the incarnational design of life. When we consent to and cooperate with how God desires to dwell in and through us, God's dream of salvation is made real in everyday life through this holy partnership. As we participate fully in the life of God as God desires, we experience the thrill of heartfelt communion with the living God and blossom into who we are to bless the world.

Experiencing communion with God

The greatest thrill available to us as humans is the experience of heartfelt communion with the living God. Life offers not just the occasional, fleeting moments of oneness with God, as when we witness a sunset over the ocean or enjoy an unexpected intimate exchange with a passing stranger. Because God is constantly inbreaking into historical circumstances, there is a perpetual opportunity for conscious encounter with God. With time and practice, we can become increasingly perceptive of and familiar with the unmistakable sensations of the inbreaking of God's presence. As we sharpen our awareness, our time spent in heartfelt communion with God significantly grows.

This experience of love with God is not something we must earn, nor is it something we can force or manufacture by trying to manipulate God into acting in a certain way. Rather, the experience of God's love and care is pure gift, initiated by God and freely available to each of us by virtue of our humanity. Our task is to simply make ourselves available to receive all that God desires to give, to rest in the confidence that God desires to be known by us and so will reveal God's self in order to draw us into loving companionship.

Through this ongoing encounter with God, we become a communion of persons. Creature and Creator are knit together by the Holy Spirit into a new creation. This is trinitarian life: two become one, each pouring themselves out in service and love to the other, which through the power of the Holy Spirit creates a third entity—a dynamic living communion of persons. As our spiritual life deepens, we come to a point where we can no longer determine where we end and where the living God begins. Each communion between creature and Creator is forged in the depths of God's heart and cannot be replicated in time or history. In this way, every life is sacred, irreplaceable to God and to the world. "For it was you who formed my inward parts; you knit me together in my mother's womb. I praise you, for I am fearfully and wonderfully made. Wonderful are your works; that I know very well" (Psalm 139:13-14).

It is this understanding of life that animates the devotion many Christians have to preventing abortion, and why some cannot abide it even in cases of rape. Abortion is an extraordinarily complex issue with many powerful, intersecting forces, including an entrenched misogyny that seeks only to control women's bodies and enslave them to the domestic sphere; a pernicious sexism that values the lives of babies over and above mothers; the fundamentalist Christian movement to oppose the use of any and all contraception; a throwaway culture where life of all kinds is degraded, objectified, and exploited; a secular culture of promiscuity that lauds sex without connection or consequence; a culture of violence against women that permits everything from rape and murder to the easy abandonment of families by fathers; a broken economic system that refuses basic human rights like healthcare, safe housing, decent education, and a living wage. However, among these dark forces shines a thread of true light: that every life is irreplaceable with its own unique share in the life of God, and so has the right to fully participate in this life with God according to God's desires.

The experience of conscious encounter with God is not offered to mystics alone but is available to everyone by virtue of our humanity. It is an unparalleled experience to feel loved and accepted just as we are by the One who created us. We do not need to earn this love: it is freely and faithfully given, regardless of what we have or have not done. As captured in the parable of the prodigal son (Luke 15:11-32), God never abandons us, always relentlessly seeking to bring us to fullness of life.

Within such an understanding, the death penalty is a profound betrayal of God. While it may understandably bring some sort of satisfaction or relief to the devastated families who can never get their loved ones back, capital punishment inherently violates God's commitment of love. No one is a lost cause to God: it is never too late for a life to be redeemed, renewed, transformed, and we are not to deny this possibility in anyone's life— this is beyond our realm of authority. How might life together be different if the justice and prison systems were rooted in God's mercy—redesigned with healing and reconciliation at the center rather than punishment and retribution? "Go and learn what this means, 'I desire mercy, not sacrifice'" (Matthew 9:13). It is easy to lock people up and throw away the key, for then we do not have to change as a society; we do not need to acknowledge the root problems that produce widespread crime and violence. We do not need to do the hard work of reorganizing our world.

The experience of heartfelt oneness with the living God is the most fulfilling, joyous experience available to us as humans, and we rejoice. This rejoicing is not ours alone, but also God's. When we are drawn by the Holy Spirit into communion with God, God swells with pleasure for God constantly pines for us, longs for us, waits eagerly for our conscious recognition. When we finally become aware of God, God burns in ecstasy as this share of God's dream comes to fulfillment. God delights in this experience of communion with us, and it is our great privilege to give God joy.

Becoming who we are

As we experience ongoing encounter with God, we are swept up by the Holy Spirit onto a never-ending journey of becoming. The more we come to know God, the more we come to know ourselves—who we are as a human person, who we are for God. God's presence is so pure that it transforms us, and we begin to see and experience life differently: we begin to experience life through the heart of God.

As we continue to journey together with God, the Holy Spirit guides us into ever-new expressions of our deepest self as God's creation. God prunes us, plunging us into a river of transformation—inviting us to shed over and over the snakeskins of what binds us to become a new creation. As we submit to this pruning, we discover the surprising depths and colors and frontiers hidden within us.

We see this dynamic of becoming in the life of Malcolm X. Born Malcolm Little, he experienced serious hardship in his early life. His father died violently when he was six, and though ruled an accident, many suspected his father was murdered by white supremacists. His mother was subsequently hospitalized, forcing young Malcolm into a series of foster homes and stints living with family. At 21 he ended up in prison, where he met the living God through the Muslim faith. A total transformation took place through encounter with God, and he began to understand who he was for God, as well as the vision of flourishing that God had for Black people in America. His journey of blossoming in the light of God continued for many years, including a particularly eye-opening pilgrimage to Mecca about a year before his devastating murder in 1965. The life of Malcolm X reveals the fundamental paradox of a life in God: the more we give ourselves over to God, the more authentically ourselves we become.

Even as blessings abundantly overflow along the path of our becoming, the journey at times can be one of great struggle. We experience the relentless invitation to let go of worldly attachments, to be perpetually dislocated by the Holy Spirit in those places within us that need fresh air and light. This pruning is not about performance or earning God's approval, but quite the opposite: God accepts us as we are and desires to free us of our pain—the pain inflicted upon us by the world, the pain we inflict on others, the pain we inflict upon ourselves. Jesus speaks of his own experience of being pruned by God: "I am the true vine, and my Father is the vinegrower. He removes every branch in me that bears no fruit. Every branch that bears fruit he prunes to make it bear more fruit" (John 15:1-2). God is always offering us more healing, more fullness of life, and greater freedom to become who we are in God.

We can see this letting-go-to-become dynamic in anyone who enters recovery from addiction. They must let go of the substance that grips them, of self-hatred, of failures and grudges and mistakes, of the deep wounds, especially those they received early in life. Whether it is addiction, eating disorders, sadism, pedophilia, self-injury, or any number of things, all of us have inner wounds from which disordered prisons of self-hatred take root and grow up within us, choking out the goodness that God intends for our lives. It is from this self-imprisonment that God wants to free us.

Still, as much as we might want to be free, it is quite difficult at times to let go—even when we know it is the best thing for us, even as we grow in deeper trust and communion with God, even as our self-discovery continues to surprise and delight us. In these times of struggle, we are often tempted to cling to what is familiar, but it is only in the letting go that we can embrace the fullness of life that God desires for us. "Unless a grain of wheat falls into the earth and dies, it remains just a single grain; but if it dies, it bears much fruit" (John 12:24). As we let go—that is, die to the self as we are—we are freed to become. As we are freed, then, we can more fully live our lives in our service of others. Thus, as challenging as it may be at times, we embrace the yoke of our becoming, not only for our own flourishing but for God and God's creation.

Making real God's dream of salvation

In our blossoming, we are naturally drawn by the Holy Spirit into God's project of salvation on earth. Indeed, this is the hallmark of true becoming: it orients us more fully towards others—to creating a world where others, too, can become according to God's desires. The more we honor the invitations of God's Holy Spirit, the more we blossom into sources of God's mercy and comfort, into instruments of reconciliation and hope, into agents of challenge to injustice and harm. In our becoming we are joined by the power of the Holy Spirit to the Grand Becoming—God's alternate future of goodness erupting into the present moment.

This is one way to understand the call in scripture to make straight the way of the Lord (Isaiah 40:3). As we allow ourselves to be pruned of attachments and wounds, our capacity to bear the incarnational flow of God's self-expression is greatly expanded. Similar to how light shines more fully and clearly through a window once any dirt is wiped clean, when we are internally pruned and healed, the Holy Spirit can more fully course through us, giving God more room to move and express God's self. Through our willingness to let go of spiritual attachments, we make straight the way of God's inbreaking into the world.

We see the dynamic of cooperation in God's project of goodness on earth in the life of Marsha P. Johnson, a Black transgender activist who helped ignite the modern LGBTQ movement. Assigned male at birth, Marsha was born and raised in New Jersey. She felt drawn to dresses and women's clothing as early as five years old. However, she quickly learned that expressing her true self put her in danger. After being harassed and bullied by neighborhood boys—even experiencing sexual assault at the hands of a 13-year-old boy—Marsha hid this core part of herself until adulthood. Days after graduating high school, she relocated to New York City with $15 and a bag of clothing.

Welcomed into the city's vibrant queer community, Marsha boldly claimed her identity and blossomed into her truest self. She further evolved into a devoted activist for the LGBTQ community. She stood on the frontlines of the Stonewall uprising in 1969, and she subsequently co-founded Street Transvestite Action Revolutionaries (STAR) with Sylvia Rivera in 1970, a nonprofit that offered shelter and care to homeless queer youth, with a special focus on trans women of color excluded from mainstream gay rights spaces. Marsha was a fierce advocate for the trans community until her tragic death in 1992 at age 46. Though it was ruled a suicide, her community suspected foul play, but the police refused to investigate further. Marsha's journey of becoming culminated in her work of creating spaces for others who were banished to the margins of the margins—spaces that offered safety so that they, too, could blossom into who they were. Put simply, Marsha devoted her becoming to the becoming of others. This is what it looks like to cooperate with God to make real God's salvation in the present moment.

Marsha P. Johnson, Malcolm X, Milo Runkle, Scott Harrison: each of their stories highlights an absolutely essential aspect of God's salvation. It is not merely spiritual, but also physical—it includes the well-being of bodies, not just souls. Indeed, Jesus is not only a teacher of faith and morals: he is the healer of bodies that suffer under the crushing weight of illness (John 5:1-8); he is the reconciler who brings bodies cast onto the margins back into communion with families and neighbors (Luke 5:12-14); he is the liberator who proclaims freedom from poverty and oppression (Luke 4:18); he is the reformer who challenges the abuse of power by hypocritical leadership (Mark 12:38-40). The God of the Bible is not only concerned with spiritual salvation, but with the flourishing of the whole person. We cannot claim fidelity to God unless we work for the totality of salvation for all creation.

***

When we recognize the incarnational design of life, we can begin to see why honoring God's inbreaking into history matters—how every life is important to all other life, irrespective of wealth or social position or power. What is the fruit of honoring God's inbreaking into your own life? What blessings do you experience, and how do you make real God's goodness for others? With some imagination we can glimpse the infinite goodness that is possible if humanity were to fully cooperate with the incarnational design of life. Yet, we do not cooperate: as a species we refuse our consent on a grand scale, especially by erecting institutions that all too often obstruct God's incarnational initiative rather than facilitate it, thereby causing great harm to humanity and all creation.

+

PART TWO:
INSTITUTIONAL OBSTRUCTION

"This world is rigged with ruin."

—Kevin Young

Engaging with Part Two

At times institutions do facilitate the inbreaking of God into historical circumstances, such as when governments protect civil rights or monitor the safety of food or protect consumers from predatory lending practices. At other times institutions work directly against God. Part Two investigates the latter to gain insight into how to overcome this obstruction when it shows up in our lives. Chapter 4 examines some crucial techniques institutions use to interfere in the life of God. Chapter 5 identifies several symptoms that indicate the presence of obstruction in our lives. Chapter 6 considers the cost we pay as a result of the institution's misalignment with God. While institutions employ obvious savage tactics of obstruction, such as war, slavery, poverty, and all manner of violence, these chapters investigate the subtler techniques that often underpin and justify these more brutal tactics of institutional obstruction in the life of God.

4 | TECHNIQUES

God gives humanity the great and terrifying power to obstruct God's inbreaking into the world. This is, indeed, a puzzling aspect of reality: we have been granted the mysterious freedom to reject God, to frustrate the full range of God's self-expression, to delay the entrance of goodness into the present moment. While institutions at times can and do cooperate with God's incarnational initiative, too often they do not, and as a result, cause profound harm to humanity and creation. While institutions use ruthless techniques like militarized violence and harsh oppression, they must also employ subtler techniques to legitimize and make possible those more vicious tactics.

The narrowing of possibility

Anita Yellowhair was ten years old in 1950 when she was forced by the federal government onto a bus and relocated with hundreds of other Indigenous children to Intermountain Indian School, the largest Indian residential school in the United States. Her mother, father, and grandparents could only helplessly watch as the government forcibly separated her from her family, her culture, her people.

Intentional family separation through Indian boarding schools was implemented in the U.S. from 1860 to 1978. This policy was motivated by the 1819 Indian Civilization Act, which enshrined into law the goal of total eradication of Indigenous culture by "civilizing" them with white culture. The Christian Church—Protestant and Catholic—had a prominent role in assisting with the government's dark mission.

These schools had strict rules, especially regarding the use of native languages, which were enforced through harsh punishment like solitary confinement, the withholding of food, and physical violence like whipping and slapping. In addition, physical and sexual abuse of children by staff was rampant. "[D]o not oppress the widow, the orphan, the alien, or the poor; and do not devise evil in your hearts against one another. But they refused to listen, and turned a stubborn shoulder, and stopped their ears in order not to hear" (Zechariah 7:10-11). Indeed, those in federal and Christian leadership stopped up their ears to the cry of the Indigenous peoples: by 1978, the U.S. federal government established 357 schools across 30 states to separate approximately 60,000 children from their families—a complete betrayal of God.

The treatment of Indigenous peoples by the U.S. federal government illustrates one of the most prominent and effective strategies of institutional obstruction in the life of God: the narrowing of possibility—that is, restricting at the outset which people can be incarnational pathways for God's inbreaking and which people cannot. This narrowing happens at the level of category, where the institution defines which people can fully participate in the life of God and how they are permitted to do so. While St. Paul boldly abolishes categories—"there is no longer Jew or Greek, there is no longer slave or free, there is no longer male and female; for all of you are one in Christ Jesus" (Galatians 3:28)—institutions often establish ways of proceeding from narrow categories that facilitate, sanction, and empower the full participation of some, but not others, in the life of God. Instead of grace being initiated by God, the institution steps in to ration goodness according to its own definitions of reality.

Through the narrowing of possibility, there is an imposition of the bleak where circumstances are presented to the people as unchanging and unchangeable. The institution projects a stance of certainty, rooted in a false claim that there is nothing more to learn, nothing more to discover. Life's ordering is made simple with all mystery removed, which shrinks the collective imagination of what is possible. The current circumstances are presented as final with no hope of an alternate future—a convincing deception that induces a sense of despair, numbness, or resignation in the subjugated people. Circumstances appear insurmountable, even beyond the reach of God.

The reasons offered by the institution to justify this narrowing of possibility—why some are allowed to participate in the life of God while others are not—ring hollow in light of a loving God who promises fullness of life for all: "I came that they may have life, and have it abundantly" (John 10:10). There is an abrasive dissonance between the goodness that God intends for us and the claims being made by the institution. There is also frequently an internal contradiction between the actions of the institution and its declared mission and values—a hypocrisy that results from lack of integrity.

The narrowing of possibility inscribes and enforces margins, uplifting some lives at the expense of others. In this way, the institution must be willing to create victims in order to uphold its narrow definitions of reality. These boundaries are then policed not only by official mechanisms, but by any willing participant within the institution. At times this peer surveillance is done in earnest with love for the institution, but far more often it sprouts from fear, rigidity, or the desire to maintain power and control. Policing tactics can range from verbal violence like insults and harassment, to physical violence and official institutional punishment, to even death. The goal of the surveillance is to guard the narrow definitions of reality upon which the institution's self-understanding and ways of proceeding are built, which insulates the institution from the destabilizing effects of God's Holy Spirit. Such policing breeds fear and conformity, creating an environment that makes it even harder for possibility to emerge.

Patriarchy relies very heavily on the narrowing of possibility. This is laid bare in the manosphere, an online world that narrows possibility not only for women, who are deemed naturally inferior and thus worthy of subjugation, but also for men, who must inhabit a profoundly restricted interpretation of masculinity or be outcast. Patriarchy's gender ideology, which in varying degrees permeates across religions and cultures, intensely restricts God's creative self-expression within and through humanity.

Importantly, men—who also suffer under patriachy—are not the problem, but rather the broad agreement of societies to organize themselves into hierarchies where only a certain limited expression of manhood is valued and accepted. This restrictive social agreement inherently degrades and invalidates all other expressions of gender and sexuality as lesser and secondary, even those of men who fall beyond their rigid definitions. In the case of the manosphere, members use shame and humiliation to viciously surveil one another's expression of masculinity, taking issue with any behavior or body type that does not meet the concept of the "alpha" male.

To successfully narrow possibility, the institution must dismiss those pushed out by the narrowing. As far as the institution is concerned, no authority resides in the voices of the marginalized: they are infantilized, robbed of any credibility. Assuming their incompetence in knowing God's desires for their lives, the institution steps in to dictate outcomes for them like a parent does a child. Those pushed to the margins might internalize the limits placed upon them by the institution, which kills dreams and vitality before they can even take root.

This institutional grip on reality suppresses the healthy push-pull dialogue that is needed for the whole community to flourish. This give-and-take dynamic where everyone has something to learn can only unfold when all participants of the institution are regarded as both teachers and learners. However, when possibility is narrowed and the definitions of reality are presented as indisputable, the institution's rigidity and tight claim on truth obstructs the fullness of God's creative inbreaking. As a result, the institution stagnates under the weight of its status quo.

Manipulation of process

Another way that institutions obstruct God's incarnational initiative is by manipulating processes to lead to a pre-determined outcome. In these situations, the process is presented as open on its face, but this openness is in word only. Beneath the veneer is an agenda that is committed to delivering a desired outcome that upholds the institution's existing state and cements its power. Similar to the technique of narrowing possibility, the manipulation of process also prevents the free and authentic grappling required to uncover how God desires to move in and through God's people. Instead of affording God the time and space to communicate and lead, the conclusion is reached before the process starts, obstructing the full agency of the Holy Spirit and making the process a farce.

Boeing's handling of the 737 MAX stands as a stark example of the manipulation of process with catastrophic consequences. In an effort to rush the aircraft to market, Boeing downplayed the significance of the new Maneuvering Characteristics Augmentation System (MCAS) software, presenting it to regulators as a minor adjustment rather than a significant safety-critical feature. The company was able to avoid triggering more rigorous certification requirements that could have delayed the plane's rollout and required additional training for pilots. Investigations eventually surfaced that Boeing pressured the Federal Aviation Administration to delegate much of the safety oversight back to the company itself, effectively allowing Boeing to certify its own work. This manipulation of regulatory processes contributed directly to two crashes—Lion Air Flight 610 in 2018 and Ethiopian Airlines Flight 302 in 2019—that killed 346 people. "My eyes flow with rivers of tears because of the destruction of my people. My eyes will flow without ceasing, without respite, until the Lord from heaven looks down and sees" (Lamentations 3:48-50).

Such manipulation of process is rampant across society. We see it in the practice of gerrymandering and all manner of voter suppression; in the manipulation of financial markets and tools that led to the 2008 U.S. financial crash; in the legislation that criminalizes homelessness and mental illness so we as a society can avoid doing the work of addressing root causes. This tactic was used in the recent abuse of the federal budget reconciliation process where the Republican-led U.S. Congress not only clawed back billions of dollars already allocated through past bipartisan legislation, but also secured the largest wealth transfer from the poor to the rich in U.S. history—a fact the politicians themselves seem to understand since they delayed the implementation of the austerity measures until after the 2026 election. "Ah, you who make iniquitous decrees, who write oppressive statutes, to turn aside the needy from justice and to rob the poor of my people of their right, that widows may be your spoil, and that you may make the orphans your prey" (Isaiah 10:1-2). The powerful are especially adept at manipulating processes to enrich themselves at the expense of the vulnerable, something repeatedly condemned by the prophets in the Hebrew scriptures (Amos 5:11; Micah 3:9-11; Ezekiel 22:29; Jeremiah 22:13).

At times the lack of openness is not necessarily conscious or malicious. It can sprout up from a love of longheld beliefs or traditions, from the desire for integrity in mission and values, or from an honest devotion to the institution. Regardless, when processes are manipulated to reach a pre-determined outcome, deep spiritual attachment is in play. At best there is a lack of interior freedom, at worst a nefarious motivation rooted in greed and power. As a result, the institution pushes the waters in a certain direction rather than trusting the movements of the Spirit to flow to a new, perhaps unexpected, destination. Such attachment to the way things are impedes any opportunity for true discovery precisely because the full range of God's self-communication is prevented from entering.

There may be times when an institution-al process begins in true openness, but as it starts to point to an unexpected outcome, the leadership becomes spooked and interrupts or redirects the process before it can freely unfold to its honest conclusion. This obstruction is an artificial force imposed upon the process from above, rather than a genuine movement that arises from below. The imposition is accompanied by a willingness to violate the institution's most highly regarded values so as to maintain control over reality. Such manipulation deforms the institution's integrity and elicits a sense of betrayal in the hearts of participants, damaging at a fundamental level—sometimes permanently—their respect and devotion.

Such manipulation of process unfolded during the Roman Catholic Church's recent Synod on Synodality, a three-year consultative process launched by Pope Francis in 2021 to give Catholics in the pews the opportunity to voice their prayerful feedback to the institutional Church. Synodality, a way of proceeding reclaimed from the early Church through the Second Vatican Council, encourages prayerful listening, open dialogue and participation at all levels of Church life to uncover the invitations of God's Holy Spirit. As this three-year process unfolded, the role of women in the Church was one of the most acute issues to arise. The call to ordain women as deacons consistently surfaced throughout all phases of consultation (the ordination of women as priests also consistently arose, though not universally).

By the start of the Synod in 2021, Francis himself—in both word and deed—had long indicated that the teaching on women in the diaconate was open for discernment. However, he showed conflicting movements. On the one hand, Francis established commissions in 2016 and 2020 to study the possibility of a "female diaconate," studies whose findings were never released. On the other hand, he consistently remarked that the sacrament of ordination for women as deacons (or priests) was not possible, while later adding that a female diaconate might perhaps be envisioned as something different from the male diaconate. Of course, with any such pre-determined limitations in place, a true discernment on the issue is not possible: the Holy Spirit requires our complete inner freedom if we are to recognize and follow where God wants to lead. While Pope Francis displayed truly remarkable inner freedom in practically all other aspects of his pontificate, he over and over evidenced that he did not have such freedom when it came to the issue of women and the sacrament of ordination.

Nonetheless, when the waters of dialogue were allowed to flow freely throughout the Church, the call for the ordination of women as deacons (and priests) continued to bubble up throughout every stage of the Synod's process, including among male deacons, priests, and bishops. While resistance was voiced by some participants, the far larger current flowing was in favor of the ordination of women as deacons. However, a few months before the conclusion of the three-year process, when hundreds of Synod delegates from all over the world were scheduled to gather in Rome for the final assembly, Pope Francis went into the U.S. media to assert that women could not now, or ever, be ordained as deacons.

This move by the Pope—intentional or not—essentially threw cold water on what was a natural unfolding of the process, which precluded any possibility of Synod delegates arriving at a different conclusion. The outcome of the Synod on a female diaconate ended where it began: somewhat open for study. "You abandon the commandment of God and hold to human tradition" (Mark

7:8). Pope Francis violated the values and process that he himself set up in order to ensure a predetermined outcome that insulated the institution from the inbreaking of God.

The refusal to admit reality

In recent years it has come to light that big oil companies have known since the 1960s that burning fossil fuels causes global warming. Using their vast fortunes, they have worked for decades to spread disinformation about this fact. They employed a loyal team of well-paid, unscrupulous scientists to spread lies and deny the science, all while spending hundreds of millions of dollars each year to aggressively lobby politicians. Their tactics have kept the public in the dark during these crucial decades, delaying the inevitable transition away from fossil fuels while bringing life on earth to the precipice of disaster. Interested in short-term selfish gains, oil companies have raked in trillions of dollars in profits. From 2021 to 2023 alone, the top five U.S.-based oil and gas companies earned record-breaking *profits of more than $250 billion*. "Alas for those who lie on beds of ivory, and lounge on their couches, and eat lambs from the flock, and calves from the stall; who sing idle songs to the sound of the harp, and like David improvise on instruments of music; who drink wine from bowls, and anoint themselves with the finest oils, but are not grieved over the ruin of Joseph" (Amos 6:4-6). Greed is a sickness that infects our spirits and prevents us from seeing through the heart of God and valuing life as God intends.

The behavior of the oil and gas industry makes visible a shrewd technique for obstructing God's incarnational initiative: the refusal to admit a factual reality that opposes the institution's way of proceeding, self-understanding, or truth claims. This tactic is frequently used for avarice, as evidenced not only by big oil's attack on science, but also by the chemical industry, which knew decades ago that dangerous forever chemicals (PFAS) were poisoning our blood, the land, and the waters, but denied this reality to protect their bottom line. Similarly, this tactic is used by the duplicitous one trillion dollar food industry, which blames the obesity and illness epidemic on individual choice and lack of exercise all while pouring hundreds of millions of dollars into designing addictive products with "bliss points" that purposefully exploit human physiology to enslave us to their nutritionally bankrupt, ultra-processed, food-like food—much of which heavily relies on the abject horrors of factory farming.

The refusal to admit reality is also an essential strategy of the Trump administration. From the denial of losing the 2020 presidential election—an election that courts have repeatedly verified as free and fair with Joe Biden as the winner—to the dismantling, weakening, or hijacking of federal agencies, the Trump administration relies heavily on reality denialism to cement and perpetuate its power. The administration aggressively attacks watchdog agencies, including the Inspectors General, Consumer Financial Protection Bureau, Consumer Product Safety Commission, Internal Revenue Service, Environmental Protection Agency, and Corporation for Public Broadcasting. It has also greatly undermined or suspended data collection, such as scientific weather and climate data, public health trends, green-house gas emissions, and statistics on labor and the economy. It is much easier to deny reality and claim that the administration's policies and decisions serve the common good when accountability mechanisms and factual data have been eradicated. "[T]heir houses are full of treachery; therefore they have become great and rich, they have grown fat and sleek. They know no limits in deeds of wickedness; they do not judge with justice the cause of the orphan, to make it prosper, and they do not defend the rights of the needy" (Jeremiah 5:27-28).

In addition to avarice, reality denialism is also used to defend institutions from the dawning awareness of a reality that points to a more expansive horizon of possibility. Because the emerging reality threatens the present order, the institution simply refuses to admit the reality exists. This tactic is commonly used by many denominations within the Christian Church in its treatment of the LGBTQ community. For example, Alana Chen, a young woman from Boulder, Colorado, had a deep devotion to her Catholic faith and a simultaneous struggle with her sexuality. As a teenager she started to seek guidance from priests and church-affiliated counselors who encouraged her to conceal her attraction to women and pursue a path of celibacy as the only acceptable option.

Over the years, this counseling, often framed in ways resembling conversion therapy, left her feeling ashamed and conflicted, forcing her to choose between her faith and her authentic self—that is, her share in the life of God. Despite her devotion to God, the pressure to suppress her identity took a devastating toll on her mental health. In December 2019, at just 24 years old, Alana died by suicide. "For the hurt of my poor people I am hurt, I mourn, and dismay has taken hold of me" (Jeremiah 8:21). While medical and social science has revealed gender expression and sexuality are quite complex, the Roman Catholic Church—and many other denominations of Christianity—continues to cling to an entrenched gender ideology that prevents it from deeper understanding of the human person. As a result, the Catholic priests and counselors who tried to minister to Alana were unable to see who she truly was. The Church is deeply implicated in the tragic death of this young woman.

A particularly effective expression of reality denialism is blame reversal—that is, when an aggressor claims victimhood to justify the victimizing of others. Perpetrators of domestic violence frequently use this tactic as they frame themselves as the real victim who is provoked into violence, thereby shifting blame onto the victims and absolving themselves of responsibility. On the institutional level, President Vladimir Putin recently used this form of reality denialism to justify the 2022 Russian invasion of Ukraine. He repeatedly invoked a false narrative claiming Ukraine is run by neo-Nazis despite the country's democratically elected government and Jewish president, Volodymyr Zelenskyy.

Reversing the blame, Putin pretends Russia is acting reluctantly in preemptive self-defense while in reality he launched a war of aggression and territorial expansion that continues to take many thousands of lives. One particularly ruthless tactic of Putin's war is the systematic kidnapping of tens of thousands of Ukrainian children who are taken into Russia, naturalized, and placed with Russian families or in camps—a sinister attempt to break the spirit of the people while also destroying the children's Ukrainian identity. "How sick is your heart, says the Lord God, that you did all these things" (Ezekiel 16:30).

Reality denialism can have multiple interlocking layers that create a fortress of interwoven protection against the inbreaking of God because they are very difficult to challenge at one time. We see this complexity in the Roman Catholic Church's treatment of women and the sacrament of ordination. There are two ordination tracks in the Church: one for deacons and one for priests. Each ordained role has different responsibilities that flow from different theologies. At the risk of oversimplifying, the Second Vatican Council explains that the priest participates in the ministerial priesthood of Christ ("standing in" for Christ), while the deacon's role is to help the priest. In addition to differing theologies, each office has its own historical development and biblical justification.

One layer of the refusal to admit reality is that the Church denies that culture has played a central role in the exclusion of women from ordination. Culture is at play in the way scripture has been (and continues to be) interpreted to justify male-only ordination; in the prejudiced views of women and women's bodies; and in the erasure of the history of how women participated as deacons and priests down through the centuries even in the face of such prejudice. In addition, culture is embedded within the scripture itself, a fact the institutional Church acknowledges in its recent documents on scripture, yet fails to take into account when interpreting scripture on women's roles in the Church.

One example of culture impacting biblical interpretation is the institutional Church's claim that Jesus' choice of the 12 apostles is the mandate for a male-only priesthood. This interpretation elicits the question: why is it only the maleness that matters? The apostles were also Jews, not Gentiles, and there were 12—a number deeply significant for the Jewish Jesus as it references the 12 tribes of Israel. If Jesus' choice of apostles is the mandate for priesthood, then why doesn't the Catholic Church have 12 male Jews as priests? All of today's thousands of priests, save a handful of Jewish converts, would be disqualified from ordination on the grounds they are Gentiles. "Isaiah prophesied rightly about you hypocrites, as it is written, 'This people honors me with their lips, but their hearts are far from me; in vain do they worship me, teaching human precepts as doctrines'" (Mark 7:6-7). The institutional Church extracted the one characteristic of the 12 that justifies the Church's current way of proceeding—a biblical interpretation that violates the Gospel's core message of fullness of life for all people.

A second layer of reality denialism in the Church's treatment of the ordination of women is that the institutional Church must deny that the doctrine of ordination is open for discernment. This is true in the general sense that everything is always open for discernment because we are limited human beings in relationship with a teaching God who desires to continually free us from our blindness and bring us to greater insight. But the doctrine on ordination is also open for discernment in that there is increasing support in many countries for the ordination of women both as deacons and priests, and this support exists at every level of the Church, including among male deacons, priests, and bishops. In particular, the divergence among bishops means that they are no longer in communion, which—according to the documents of the Second Vatican Council—indicates the teaching cannot be definitively held. However, the Church denies this reality, pretending that because the practice of male-only ordination has been ongoing for many years that this inherently means the teaching must be in alignment with God. However, we all know this is not necessarily the case: injustice can be carried out for centuries—as in the case of chattel slavery in the U.S.—before people finally awaken to its misalignment with God.

A third layer of reality denialism is the institutional Church's pretense that its form and way of proceeding are eternal and unchanging—that it never evolves or develops in any way. This sleight of hand makes Catholics generally unprepared for the natural unfolding of tradition that happens when in relationship with an infinite, teaching God. As historians know well, the Church has evolved greatly in structure, tradition, and its many theologies over two thousand years of existence, growing from a fledgling movement of Judaism into a global empire. The Church has even reversed doctrine at times, including its stance on religious freedom, the treatment of the Jews, and whether truth resides in other religions. The Church evolves as it continues to strive to understand the eternal God. By denying this reality and misrepresenting itself as unchanging, the Church makes its necessary pruning that much more difficult.

These interlocking layers of reality denialism have been formidable in protecting the Church's status quo on ordination. However, we are now seeing some cracks. In recent decades the pressure on the Catholic Church to ordain women has been mounting, perhaps due to a mix of factors, including the general awakening to women's equality happening throughout the world, the increasing shortage of male priests, and the horrific revelations of the widespread sexual abuse scandal, where male priests sexually assaulted children and were protected by male bishops. Whatever the reasons, the institutional Church is now, as mentioned, conceding that a female diaconate is "open for study," though exactly what this means is unclear since the sacrament of ordination itself appears to be off the table.

While the Church has stated that a female diaconate can be studied, it has stood firm that priesthood is still closed. This move has split ordination into two separate issues: one that is open for discussion (deacons) and one that is not (priests). This strategy employs a fourth layer of reality denialism: by dividing the issue this way, the Church pretends that the institution is the source of vocation and that it has the power to determine which categories of people are entitled to invitations from God and which are not. However, vocation does not come from the Church—it comes from God *through* the Church. It is the institution's moral responsibility to ensure that it properly recognizes and honors how God desires to move in and through its members.

The Church's false split of the issue of sacramental ordination has created a division among the movements that support the participation of women in the Church, successfully undermining them. There are some who accept the Church's framing as valid and so advocate for the ordination of women as deacons but not as priests, which—intentionally or unwittingly— colludes with and legitimizes the multiple layers of the Church's reality denialism.

Though it is politically expedient to honor the all-male leadership's approach to the issue, this expediency comes at a steep cost. While there is no doubt that the

Church would greatly benefit from the gifts of female deacons (whatever their responsibilities), if women are welcomed as deacons but not priests, these female deacons would be vulnerable to an all-male authority with a long history of denigrating women's bodies and exploiting women's labor. Indeed, the sexual abuse scandal is still ongoing: nuns in India and Africa are reporting pervasive rape by male priests with little response from male bishops. How would a subcaste of female deacons be protected within this patriarchal structure?

Further, the Church will get to claim progress, which will significantly diminish the pressure needed to bring the Church into alignment with God on its treatment of women. The opportunity of the historical moment will be squandered, and true justice for women in the Church will be set back for centuries. "If a kingdom is divided against itself, that kingdom cannot stand. And if a house is divided against itself, that house will not be able to stand" (Mark 3:24-25). When we buy into reality denialism on the part of any institution, it creates additional harm. Thus, the path to justice for women in the Catholic Church is a united, uncompromising movement that stands together as one body to compel the institutional Church to fully confront reality and do what is right.

Whether any particular institution's denial of reality is calculated or unconscious, it always perpetuates a delusion that things can and will remain the same—that the institution is always, already right, and that circumstances are unchanging and unchangeable. In these instances, the institution has no curiosity, no openness, no humility, no willingness to confront what is factually true. Any voices that embody or validate the rising reality are ignored, erased, dismissed, or silenced. If somehow voices break through, the institution attacks them by demonizing them as dangerous and unfaithful to the institution.

This gaslighting fractures the people by sowing confusion and division among them, which prevents them from being able to effectively respond to the institution's false narrative. It can also induce despair and a sense of inner diminishment of something deep within the hearts of those affected by the reality denialism—a shrinking of the self that feels necessary for surviving daily life. The goal of reality denialism is to safeguard the institution and its leadership, delaying for as long as possible and at any cost the looming, inevitable inbreaking of God.

***

Institutions use these techniques—and others—to greatly obstruct God's incarnational initiative. These strategies are very effective at insulating the institution from the very inbreaking of God needed for humanity to fully flourish as God intends. Have institutions obstructed your ability to fully participate in the life of God? Institutional obstruction always leaves a pattern of symptoms in our lives that alert us to its presence. When we become aware of these symptoms, we give the Holy Spirit the opportunity to teach us how to understand what is transpiring through a spiritual lens. Gaining this insight is a key step to finding fullness of life beyond the grip of institutional obstruction.

+

5 | SYMPTOMS

When institutions obstruct God's desires for our lives, this interference produces identifiable patterns of impact in our everyday experiences. When we become conscious of these symptoms, we are alerted to the presence of institutional obstruction in our ability to fully participate in the life of God. This awareness gives God the opportunity to lead us through or around the obstruction to fullness of life, even when these barriers are formidable.

Crosscurrents that create friction

Born with spina bifida, a defect of the spinal cord, Tatyana McFadden lived in an orphanage in St. Petersburg, Russia, where she learned to "scoot" or walk on her hands before being adopted and brought to the

U.S. at the age of six. She received medical care, schooling, a wheelchair, and the opportunity to get involved in para-sports. Tatyana was supremely gifted in skill and athleticism. With a supportive family she started to blossom, winning her first Paralympic medal at age 15. Even with her talent, her school refused to allow her to compete with the other students and so her family decided to sue. The courts ruled in Tatyana's favor and Maryland schools were forced to allow students with disabilities to compete alongside their peers. Tatyana went on to become a 17-time Paralympic medalist and winner of all four major world marathons in a single year. "For surely I know the plans I have for you, says the Lord, plans for your welfare and not for harm, to give you a future with hope" (Jeremiah 29:11). Her advocacy also led to Maryland passing the first state law guaranteeing equal access to sports for students with disabilities in 2008.

A telltale symptom of institutional obstruction of God's incarnational initiative in our lives is the presence of conflicting crosscurrents between what is happening at the local/personal level versus the claims being made at the institutional level. The movements are in direct opposition to each other and so create a sense of friction in everyday life. For example, maybe we experience the repeated affirmation of our gifts for a particular path by our community of people who know us best. Perhaps opportunities that support our path continue to arise, sometimes mysteriously, though we are told by the institution we are not welcome. Maybe we experience an unshakeable inner knowing of our life's purpose that is confirmed over and over in our prayer. Perhaps all three movements—community confirmation, repeated opportunities, and inner knowing—coalesce to indicate the presence of an incarnational pathway for God's self-expression in and through us.

However, while our journey on the personal level may be deepening, the institution is inserting itself to the detriment of our progression. This external hand that hinders is impersonal; it has a certain facelessness, its source feeling far removed to a distant and unidentifiable place. It does not know us, and shows no sign of desiring to build intimacy. The external hand is disinterested, incapable, or unwilling to acknowledge our existence. Standing before this force, we typically are made to feel dismissed before we can even utter a word of our experience. If we try to authentically connect with it, we are met with a certainty that refuses to listen, a hubris that makes impossible the disposition of listening and learning needed for the true flourishing of life on earth. The hand that hinders strives to make us invisible so that no one is made aware of our story.

The sensibility between such crosscurrents is stark. Where the currents within our personal, local lives are gentle, inviting, and affirming, the currents from the institution are typically cold, uncharitable, and obstinate as the institution's authority sows doubt and discouragement, produces inner confusion and anxiety, or undermines our confidence in our own inner knowing. As in Tatyana's case, while the movements on the personal level plunge us more deeply into the river of our becoming, the movements from the institution work hard to stem this natural tide. This experience generates a sense of friction as God's Holy Spirit works to find ways around the blockade that continues to assert itself against God's inbreaking. The friction may be manageable at first, but in time it often intensifies into a burden from which the soul and spirit desperately seek relief. The psalmists cry out for such rescue: "When the righteous cry for help, the Lord hears, and rescues them from all their troubles. The Lord is near to the broken-hearted, and saves the crushed in spirit" (Psalm 34:17-18).

Stagnation or redirection of our becoming

Nina Simone, born Eunice Kathleen Waymon, was performing on piano in church by the age of six. Immensely gifted, she had dreams of becoming a classical pianist. She began formal training at a young age, and with the support of white wealthy patrons who saw her promise, she attended the Allen High School for Girls, a private, integrated high school. After graduating as valedictorian, she went on to the Juilliard School in New York City with the help of a one-year scholarship. There she prepared to realize her dream as a classical pianist by attending the prestigious Curtis Institute of Music.

Despite her irrefutable talent, Nina was rejected by Curtis, an act she was certain was due to racial prejudice. This experience deeply wounded her. "Every night I flood my bed with tears; I drench my couch with my weeping. My eyes waste away because of grief; they grow weak because of all my foes" (Psalm 6:6-7). Eventually, she had to abandon her vocation as a classical pianist. She went on to reinvent herself as Nina Simone, blessing the world as a multi-genre singer, composer, and activist. While performing a mix of folk, blues, gospel, pop, and jazz, her classical background remained a central part of her identity.

Nina's story reveals another symptom of institutional obstruction of God's incarnational initiative: stagnation, which may be accompanied by forced redirection of our becoming in God. Stagnation can happen at any point along the journey. Some of us may experience momentum as we float down the river of God's Spirit until eventually it is as if a dam is met and we simply cannot go any further. Others, like those born into crushing poverty, may face massive barriers that preclude from the very start the ability to become according to God's desires.

In addition to stagnation, we may experience the forced redirection of our path. Our early journey may be progressing smoothly, but then at a certain point, try as we might, we simply cannot reach where the river wants to flow. Instead, we repeatedly find ourselves redirected to somewhere adjacent to where God calls, but never in the place itself. Importantly, as in Nina's case, this stagnation or redirection occurs through no fault of our own: we possess the inner freedom, talent, will, commitment, and drive to give ourselves over to the path of becoming, but something external is impeding us from fully doing so.

Such stagnation and redirection are often accompanied by inner frustration and a draining of vitality. God's self-expression in and through us is obstructed, and so God's Spirit grows vexed within us and we feel this frustration as our own. God's frustration incarnating within us alerts us that the institution is out of alignment with God. The pressure continues to mount as God's Holy Spirit grows increasingly frustrated. We experience the incarnational pressure building within, a fire shut up in our bones (Jeremiah 20:9), steadily and relentlessly seeking to break free.

Relationship with institution is strained

Another symptom of institutional obstruction is an increasing strain in our relationship with the offending institution. As we endure the ongoing friction of crosscurrents and the disappointment of stagnation or forced redirection, our disillusionment with the institution—a state of heart that can spill over and infect our experience of life more broadly—grows. Engagement with the institution becomes increasingly onerous and fraught with conflict, a burden we cannot seem to escape. We may feel a constant sensation of being crushed or slowly asphyxiated, worn down by the struggle imposed on us by the institution without our consent.

This strain in the relationship with one or more institutions may be something into which we are born. For example, people growing up in the Appalachian region of the U.S. are faced with poverty, food insecurity, health care deserts, under-employment and low-wage jobs, environmental hazards, lack of infrastructure, and disinvestment in education—among other challenges. In other situations, the strain with the offending institution may not be present at first but arise with time. In these cases, the relationship with the institution that was once fulfilling transforms, sometimes by surprise, into one of tension and alienation. We see this dynamic of strain in the Book of Acts as the apostles grow a significant following only to come under increasing scrutiny of the religious leadership of the time (i.e., Acts 4:1-21; Acts 5:12-42).

This experience of institutional strain is a common experience for women across religious traditions who are called to serve in ordained ministry. Frequently they become aware of and grow in their vocation to leadership within their beloved tradition, until at some point they are finally prevented from fulfilling God's dream for them by theologized sexism. This creates enormous strain on what was once a lifegiving relationship. When the situation ultimately becomes untenable, the women often must leave their home tradition to find one that honors and welcomes their vocation.

The experience of this strain on the relationship with the institution emerges first from the incarnational frustration—that is, the vexation of God's Holy Spirit as it is prevented from the full self-expression that God desires. This vexation of the Spirit then arouses emotional and psychological anguish. In this way, the strain does not result from surface annoyance, but from suffering at the deepest level of self, meaning, and purpose. This strain with the institution generates an erosion of trust, a loss of faith, a deep suspicion, and profound disillusionment in the institution—a betrayal from which it is difficult to recover.

When we are at odds with an institution that has an outsized ungodly role in our lives, the strain, whether being present from the start or arising later in our journey, intensifies with time and can surge in moments of discord. At some point we are likely to find ourselves standing bewildered before the institution's harsh obstruction and its acute impact on us. "Save me, O God, for the waters have come up to my neck. I sink in deep mire, where there is no foothold; I have come into deep waters and the flood sweeps over me. I am weary with my crying; my throat is parched. My eyes grow dim with waiting for my God" (Psalm 69:1-3). It is at this point that we often feel forced by the institution into contemplating how to deal with the obstruction, perhaps resorting to bargaining with God, scheming in our daydreams, railing in anger against the present circumstances, or wrestling with the temptations of resignation and despair.

Because it is beyond our power to remove the institutional obstruction in the moment, we wrestle with how to continue our journey. Do we endure the place of stagnation and make the best of it? Do we look for a place adjacent to God's intentions so that we can at least partially become who we are as God intends? Do we abandon our right to a particular incarnational pathway and find a different life altogether? Do we stand and fight for our right to live as God intends, and if so, how? Each person impacted by the institutional obstruction in their share in the life of God must find their own way in, around, or through the obstruction by the light of the Holy Spirit. As the life of Nina Simone illustrates, these are typically deeply painful decisions that require the difficult letting go of the dreams of how life might have been, if only the institution were in alignment with God.

***

When institutions obstruct God's incarnational initiative, the interference creates telltale symptoms that alert us to the misalignment with God's dream of a world that works for all. Are you experiencing any symptoms of obstruction in your everyday life? If so, what are they? Once we identify the symptoms, we must confront the price we pay as individuals and as a society as a result of the obstruction. This cost of suffering is best understood through the lens of the crucifixion.

+

6 | COST

When institutions obstruct God's incarnational inbreaking, they cause immense untold cost to human life and creation. It is helpful to understand this cost through the lens of crucifixion—that is, the human attempt to stop the living God from entering historical time to bring about goodness in the present moment. The crucifixion of Christ makes visible the principle of ongoing human resistance to the incarnation—that negative, often violent response to God's inbreaking that sows destruction and despair.

The crucifixion principle pervades life

After the bombing of Pearl Harbor in 1941, the United States forcibly incarcerated approximately 120,000 people of Japanese descent—about two-thirds of whom were U.S. citizens—from 1942 to 1945 under the Franklin D. Roosevelt administration. The government relocated the people to remote prison camps surrounded by barbed wire and guards. The Japanese people were incarcerated for several years under harsh conditions and so lost their homes, businesses, and livelihoods. The government justified its action as a military necessity, but no evidence of disloyalty on the part of Japanese people was ever found.

Jesus, as the revelation of the living God, makes visible not only the incarnational principle, but also the crucifixion principle, which erupts from the world. While Jesus' life and ministry communicate God's vision of fullness of life for humanity—a vision that is made real with the cooperation of the human family—his death makes clear the results of humanity's rejection of God: anguish, suffering, and death.

The dynamics of the crucifixion are, of course, captured in scripture. Jesus afflicts those in authority who cling to aspects of collective life that are out of alignment with God and so cause the suffering of those at the effect of their power (for example, Matthew

15:1-9; Matthew 23:1-36; Luke 11:37-54; John 8:12-59). The powerful regard Jesus— who is the incarnational inbreaking of the presence of the living God—as a threat to their way of proceeding, and perhaps most especially, to the benefits they receive from the current way life is organized. They do not want to change and so refuse the goodness that God is offering. They demonize the incarnation and employ whatever tactics are necessary to stamp out God's inbreaking presence. Those with authority manipulate the masses and pull the levers of power to see that Jesus is executed (Matthew 26:3-5; Matthew 26:59-60; Mark 15:11; Luke 23:1-2; John 19:12-15).

While the crucifixion of the historical Jesus was a one-time event, it reveals the underlying, ongoing reality that permeates the dynamic between God and God's people. When humanity rejects God and tries to delay or outright obliterate God's destabilizing inbreaking into history, humanity creates immense and unimaginable suffering—a refusal of the goodness that God is trying to give. This resistance to the incarnational inbreaking of God is a repudiation of the love relationship that God extends to us.

While people are no longer literally nailed to crosses, they are crucified nonetheless. Implemented on a grand scale down through time, the methods of crucifixion include emotional, psychological, and existential trauma as well as many sadistic physical and sexual violations, such as those that result from war, poverty, mass incarceration, capital punishment, human trafficking, and all manner of state-sanctioned violence. God is constantly calling humanity from such oppression and violence to God's dream of justice and flourishing on earth. This call to conversion is a constant refrain of the Hebrew prophets: "Wash yourselves; make yourselves clean; remove the evil of your doings from before my eyes; cease to do evil, learn to do good; seek justice, rescue the oppressed, defend the orphan, plead for the widow" (Isaiah 1:16-17). When will humanity awaken to God's inbreaking and embrace God's vision of flourishing?

Obstruction creates hell on earth

One of the telltale signs that an institution is out of alignment with God's incarnational initiative is that it creates victims—victims who are forced to endure an imposed literal or metaphorical death. When the crucifixion principle is active, those in power place themselves in the role of God, usurping power that is not rightly theirs in order to impose a world order that guarantees their privilege at the cost of the many. This disorder creates what is essentially a hell on earth—a realm of suffering that directly opposes and undermines God's intentions of goodness for us. Such violation of the spiritual principles that govern life can only result in terrible anguish. This anguish is the urgent alarm that the situation is far out of alignment with God and must be transformed.

Such hell on earth has been ever-present in human history: chattel slavery in the U.S., which among many other unthinkable atrocities included medical gynecological experimentation on women who were forced to submit to procedures without anesthesia; the brutal removal of the Indigenous nations to reservations, especially under President Andrew Jackson, so that the government could take possession of the land; the attempted extermination of the Jewish people by the Nazi regime in Germany, which implemented revolting and sadistic horrors that killed six million Jews; the current oppression of Palestinians in Gaza and the West Bank, where the people face extreme subjugation, intentional starvation, illegal land seizure, and human rights violations at the hands of the Israeli occupation; the unprovoked attack on Ukraine by Russia under Vladimir Putin, who has implemented the demented tactic of stealing thousands of Ukrainian children and relocating them to Russian soil; the imprisonment of the Uyghur people in the Xinjiang region of China, who are forced into labor camps and sterilized without consent; the tyrannical oppression of Afghan women born under the extreme gender ideology of the Taliban, where they are all but erased from any participation in civil and economic life; the attack on immigrants by the Trump administration, which is rapidly expanding inhumane prison camps while simultaneously turning a blind-eye to the ways U.S. foreign policy contributes to the crisis of migration in the first place; the many millions of animals trapped in laboratories where they are reduced to objects with no share in the life of God, forced to endure abuses like mistreatment by ill-trained staff, confinement to small spaces, wounds and fractures that go unattended, all while being subjected to perpetual medical procedures and medications even when vomiting, shaking, unable to stand, or sick with high fevers, only to be euthanized without sedation. "Jesus looked around at them with anger; he was grieved at their hardness of heart" (Mark 3:5). The specific circumstances and countries and victims may change, but the principle remains the same: crucifixion creates hell on earth.

Abortion, too, is a hell on earth. Apart from the termination of pregnancy due to health concerns, this issue frequently results from what might be called a trickle-down crucifixion. Women across the world are an intensely oppressed group—sexually violated, politically and theologically subjugated, prevented from full participation in civic and economic spheres. This ill-treatment intersects with and is amplified by other crushing crosses, like racism and poverty and war—which altogether creates a world hostile to the inbreaking of new life. To use the law alone to police abortion in this context of oppression is a profound hypocrisy that multiplies the crucifixion that women endure. If flourishing is desired for life in the womb, then it must also be desired for women: abortion can only be properly addressed by a total re-organization of society where the needs of women—not men—are placed at the center of civic and economic life.

The death of Jesus reveals that, for some mysterious reason, God asks our consent in making God's dream of salvation a reality. God does not and will not force us: if goodness is to reign on earth, we must choose it—we must choose to engineer our personal and collective lives to facilitate the inbreaking of God. As Moses implores, "I have set before you life and death, blessings and curses. Choose life so that you and your descendants may live" (Deuteronomy 30:19). Importantly, if we refuse to cooperate with the incarnational design of life, this does not mean, of course, that the governing spiritual principles are suspended. As with laws of physics, these spiritual principles continue to operate, whether or not we acknowledge them. When we design life to be in harmony with them, God is better able to pour God's self through us and into materiality. Indeed, this is what God keeps trying to get us to understand: if we respect God's design of life, then we as a human family can experience all the goodness that God is offering.

Often it is misconceived that this hell on earth is God's way of punishing us for our infidelity. While there are indeed mysterious tragedies like natural disasters and disease that we cannot satisfactorily explain through the lens of a loving God, the vast majority of suffering is caused by humanity's refusal to respect and cooperate with the incarnational design of life. When we fail to observe the governing principles of life, we produce widespread and severe anguish. This is not punishment: it is self-inflicted crucifixion. As the death of Jesus reveals, it is not only humanity that suffers, but also God at the hands of God's own creation. It is a great mystery as to why God permits and endures this treatment from humanity.

The institutional obstruction of God's incarnational initiative not only creates hell on earth for the crucified, it also morally maims all humanity. The ongoing obstruction numbs our collective conscience and conditions us at best to tolerate and at worst to enable and celebrate the obstruction. Suffering becomes normalized, eroding our ability to see the inherent sanctity of all living things. Some who benefit from the crucifixion are often seduced into complacency, denial, or active complicity, while others are too scared to risk their own safety to speak out against the crucifixion. In this way, institutional obstruction disfigures us all, preventing us as a human family from becoming who we truly are as God's creation and flourishing as God intends.

Untold loss of goodness ungiven

On March 6, 2024, Shaima al-Sawaf lost 50 members of her family in a single devastating Israeli missile strike on their home in Gaza. After the bombardment, a cousin's phone call to her home in Jordan delivered the unbearable news. She described herself screaming in despair, followed by a complete nervous breakdown. Among the dead were her father, mother, four brothers, one sister-in-law, and five nieces and nephews, the youngest only 18 months old. Shaima lives each day haunted by memories of her family.

Many families in Gaza are suffering a similar fate in the latest iteration of war that erupted after the gruesome October 7th attack on Israel in 2023, during which

Hamas killed approximately 1200 people and kidnapped more than 240 hostages—some of whom are tragically still in captivity. The response from the Israeli government to the attack has been disproportionate. As of August 2025, it is estimated that at least 84,000 people in Gaza have been killed (though some speculate that losses are many thousands greater if bodies under the rubble are counted), 83% of whom are civilians, the majority women and children. Thousands of children have had one or more limbs amputated and half a million Palestinians are facing famine as a result of the Israeli government's blockade of food and medicine.

In addition, while the Israeli government prevents independent journalists from entering Gaza to document the war, more than 200 Palestinian journalists have been killed by Israeli forces—a number that totals more than the number of journalists killed in the U.S. Civil War, World Wars I and II, the Vietnam War, the Korean War, the Yugoslav Wars, the Iraq War, and the War in Afghanistan combined. Further, 70% of all structures in Gaza have been destroyed, including 100% of universities, 94% of hospitals, and 92% of housing. Hundreds of cultural heritage sites and two of the four museums have also been bombed. The Israeli government has turned Gaza into a hell on earth. "My God, my God, why have you forsaken me" (Matthew 27:46).

Any such devastation on earth reveals that, in addition to the immense, heartrending cost of suffering and death caused by the crucifixion principle, there is also the profound, untold loss of talent and love and gifts that results when the crucified peoples are prevented from fully becoming who they in God. Vocations go unanswered or undiscovered; incarnational gifts go undeveloped and ungiven; relationships go unexperienced. How many works of art and literature, how many solutions to problems, how many scientific and technical advancements, how many friendships and marriages and celebrations—how much goodness has the world forfeited because of the crucifixion of God's people? In ways large and small, humanity loses out on the infinite blessings God intended these people to give to the world.

This obstruction can be felt in deeply personal ways. Each of us has been given a share of the life of God with which to bless the world. We may still be able to live out a smaller or adjacent share of God's desires, but the fullness of the life God has promised us is being denied. We are robbed of the life that God imagines for us. This unjust denial of blossoming can create deep existential suffering, forcing us to battle messages of dehumanization and resist temptations to despair. This does not mean that we are unable to experience God's incarnational initiative—we are always given by God as a gift to the world to bless it with our share in the life of God—but that the fullness of God's expression in us is unjustly taken from us. If we are victims of the crucifixion principle, we are denied the experience of blessing the world as fully as God intends and all humanity is deprived of these blessings.

It is overwhelming to begin to process the enormity of loss and suffering that we impose upon ourselves. With each person given a unique share in the life of God, these lives simply cannot be replaced—ever. This devastating institutional obstruction wreaks havoc not only on individuals but on entire groups and communities. It is unfathomable to consider not just the anguish that results from crucifixion, but the untold loss of blessings.

Forgive us, Lord, we know not what we do (Luke 23:34).

***

Have you experienced the crucifixion principle in your life? What has been the cost and how do you endure? While God mysteriously allows humanity to crucify God for a time, ultimately God's Spirit winds around and challenges all human obstruction to find expression in the world and bring about salvation. This is the resurrection principle: the faithful, unstoppability of God's inbreaking into the world to bless it with goodness.

+

PART THREE:
OVERCOMING

"A bridge of silver wings stretches from the dead ashes of an unforgiving nightmare to the jeweled vision of a life started anew."

—Aberjhani

Engaging with Part Three

Part Three investigates the ways that God overcomes institutional obstruction to enter history and bring about goodness. Chapter 7 explores the concept of the resurrection principle faithfully at work in our lives. Chapter 8 examines how God creatively navigates institutional obstruction to find alternate pathways of self-expression into the world to uplift it with goodness. Chapter 9 considers how God enters history along the path of disruption to directly challenge institutional obstruction in order to bring it into alignment with God.

7 | PREVAIL

Malala Yousafzai, born in 1997 in Pakistan, grew up with a deep love for learning that was strongly encouraged by her father. When the Taliban took control of her region and banned girls from attending school, Malala fiercely and persistently spoke out about a girl's right to education. At just 15 years old, she was shot in the head by a Taliban gunman for her advocacy. She miraculously survived. Her recovery became a global symbol of courage and she continued her fight with even greater determination. Malala became the youngest-ever Nobel Peace Prize laureate at age 17.

Resurrection as incarnational inbreaking

While it is true that institutions often obstruct God's incarnational initiative in our lives, it is also true that this grip can only be so tight. Even when institutions control circumstances, constrain opportunities for participation, and produce narrow definitions of reality, they can never entirely or permanently prevent God's inbreaking into history (Matthew 26:6; Mark 16:6; Luke 24:5-6; John 20:6-9). As Malala's life demonstrates, humanity simply does not have this ultimate power. The Taliban may claim that women and girls have no right to education, and they may even claim this position comes from God; yet, the Holy Spirit penetrates their tight grip on reality and raises up Malala to counter and lay bare their false claims. The Holy Spirit always winds around obstruction to find alternate paths of expression into the world in order to bring about goodness, to right what is wrong, to increasingly bring the world into alignment with God's project of goodness in the present moment.

This fundamental indomitability of God's Spirit is communicated to us through the resurrection of Christ. While the life of Jesus makes visible God's essential ongoing drive to incarnate into materiality, and his crucifixion humanity's resistance to God's inbreaking, the resurrection reveals God's unfailing power to overcome any obstruction that humans can possibly inflict upon God. Even humanity's most terrifying might— imperial, militarized violence—cannot halt God's entrance into history. In this way, the resurrection of Christ reveals this core essence of God's incarnational initiative: that the inbreaking of God into history cannot be ultimately prevented by humanity. In short, the resurrection reveals the unstoppability of the incarnation.

Resurrection is available to all

Because Jesus is fully human, the resurrection not only reveals God, but also humanity— that is, what is possible when humanity is disposed to God's unstoppable inbreaking into history. Through the resurrection of Jesus, God is communicating that each of us, and all humanity, can be risen by God's Holy Spirit. While the resurrection of Christ was a one-time event in history, it is revealing the hidden underlying principle that governs our life together, faithfully operating at every moment. God's Spirit is constantly seeking to enter materiality to restore us from the harm and devastation that is inflicted upon us by the world. Jesus speaks of this hidden, persistent current of renewal: "I am the resurrection and the life. Those who believe in me, even though they die, will live, and everyone who lives and believes in me will never die" (John 11:25-26). This is God's promise: to shepherd us through death into new life.

We see this dynamic of rising in the inspiring life of Dan Bigley. On July 14, 2003, Dan was walking back to his car after fishing on Alaska's Russian River when he encountered a grizzly bear with her cubs. Dan barely had time to react before she was on top of him, mauling him with a devastating force that tore his scalp, crushed his skull, and destroyed his eyes. She returned multiple times as he lay broken on the ground. Severely injured and blinded in the attack, his life came crashing down. The job he loved, his cabin in the woods, a brand new love named Amber: in the turn of one terrible moment, everything was wiped away. He was 25 years old.

Dan faced a long, excruciating recovery. He was physically alive, but lost his sight, his freedom, and his identity as an avid outdoorsman. He was plagued by a despair that enticed him to give up. Yet, somehow Dan chose to fight rather than succumb to bitterness. His grueling path required him to start over: he had to learn how to walk with a cane, navigate life without vision, and regain independence. Slowly, he discovered that his blindness did not mean the end of freedom, and with adaptation and assistance, he was eventually able to return to some of the outdoor activities he once loved. Reconnecting with Amber during his recovery, she became his wife and they had a family. He went on to earn a master's degree in social work and dedicated himself to helping others, especially youth facing challenges. "Why do you look for the living among the dead? He is not here, but has risen" (Luke 24:5). Dan ultimately reframed his blindness as a transformation of how he sees: he learned to perceive life more fully through relationships, gratitude, and a sense of purpose, which led him to a joy and resilience that he may not have otherwise discovered.

Dan's story profoundly reveals the resurrection principle at work in everyday life: no matter the circumstances, God will find a way to enter and raise us up from tragedy to fullness of life once again. God never gives up on us nor on the circumstances, however challenging they may be. We cannot understand why God permits devastating tragedy and suffering, yet we can trust that God will make us a new creation, and that this newness will be far beyond anything we can imagine. "I will cause breath to enter you, and you shall live. I will lay sinews on you, and will cause flesh to come upon you, and cover you with skin, and put breath in you, and you shall live" (Ezekiel 37:5-6). The governing spiritual reality of the resurrection principle is faithfully at work around us and in us at every moment—a reality inherent to the incarnational design of life.

Resurrection as active surrender

Importantly, the resurrection is not something that we ourselves achieve but is done unto us. Indeed, Jesus does not raise himself but *is risen* by God (Mark 16:6; Matthew 28:6; John 21:14; Romans 6:9; 1 Corinthians 15:20). To be risen from the anguish of tragedy, we must give ourselves over to the steady, unstoppable flow of God's inbreaking into time. We must allow the mystery to unfold within us: the mystery by which loss gives way to renewal, endings open into beginnings, and death becomes a seed of new creation. When we plug into God's incarnational flow, we are carried by the Holy Spirit to places beyond the limits of our imagination.

There are several facets to being risen by God's Holy Spirit. First, there is a profound letting go that must occur, an acceptance of reality. Often when we experience tragedy or crucifixion at the hands of an institution, we cling to what was or to what we want to be, resisting what actually is. Instead of clinging, we must let go and surrender to reality—a reality that is beyond our control, a reality that we deeply desire to be other than it is. This surrender does not deny grief or minimize suffering, but simply acknowledges what is real. As long as we continue to resist rather than accept the reality foisted upon us, we prevent the Holy Spirit from entering to transform us.

This is a particularly central reason as to why the United States cannot escape its deeply embedded racism. The country as a whole refuses to truly confront—fully admit and accept—the great many atrocities of its past: the brutal race-based enslavement of Black people and horrific subjugation of

Indigenous nations. Indeed, it is this refusal to admit reality that drives the Trump administration's scorched-earth assault on diversity, equity, and inclusion. This oppressive impulse is rooted in the belief that if we pretend these things didn't happen, and erase anyone and anything that points to the reality that it did, then we will flourish. But this is the exact opposite posture that the Spirit needs if we are to be washed clean and shown the way forward. "Repent and turn from all your transgressions; otherwise iniquity will be your ruin. Cast away from you all the transgressions that you have committed against me, and get yourselves a new heart and a new spirit" (Ezekiel 18:30-31). Whether as individuals, communities, or a nation, until Americans acknowledge what is real, the country will continue to refuse God's self-offering and so cannot be risen to new life as a country where all can flourish as God intends.

It is important not to conflate surrender to what is with resignation. To be risen, we must accept reality but also choose to risk hope in an alternate future. This hope comes from a deep trust in the ability of God's

Spirit to penetrate our situation and bring about healing, reconciliation, and rebirth. In this way, we must cultivate a readiness for the good: a disposition of availability to God and to God's surprises. Admittedly, this particular spiritual practice can be extraordinarily challenging in times of deep anguish. It helps to look to stories of people like Dan Bigley or Nelson Mandela or the thousands of mothers and daughters and sisters and girlfriends who have overcome breast cancer—individuals who embody the resurrection principle so profoundly that we cannot help but feel inspired to search our own lives for its presence. When we accept reality and turn toward the Holy Spirit, we provide God with the ongoing opening through which to incarnate and bring about the good.

While on the one hand we must let go and accept the present reality, on the other hand we must actively embrace our role in cooperating with God to bring new life from tragedy, from obstruction, from suffering. As Dan's incredible story reveals, there is a bedrock cooperation involved in facilitating God's inbreaking into our lives. God initiates, always initiates, but we are given the freedom to choose whether to receive and respond to what God is offering. We must be willing to turn toward God's self-gift and cooperate with what the Holy Spirit is eager to accomplish in us and for us.

In this way, God receives what we offer and multiplies it in unexpected and astonishing ways. This mysterious dynamic of multiplication is captured in scripture: the widow and the oil (2 Kings 4:1-7), Jesus feeding the five thousand (Matthew 14:13-21), Jesus' promise to Peter that the sacrifice of the twelve will be paid back one hundred fold (Mark 10:30). To embrace the incarnational design of life, we offer what we have of ourselves in any given moment and God receives it with honor, multiplies it according to God's goodness, then returns it back to us with love and joy.

For Dan, this embrace was to accept and turn toward the reality of a difficult recovery—to offer up the very depths of his being in learning to walk with a cane and navigate space without sight. Dan had to risk hope that he could participate in the activities he loved; he had to believe deep down that life could somehow be good again. "Now faith is the assurance of things hoped for, the conviction of things not seen" (Hebrews 11:1). To be risen by God we must, on the one hand, let go, and on the other, offer a total embrace. It is an active surrender: a surrender to what is and a welcome of what God will do to bring new life from the current reality.

An important aspect of this embrace is the recognition of the role that others have in our being risen by God's Holy Spirit. As mentioned, we are given as gift to one another: we are all pathways of God's incarnational inbreaking into history. Thus, God's unstoppable Spirit enters our lives through others who uplift us, minister to us, awaken us to what is possible. We see God's inbreaking in Dan Bigley's wife Amber. She did not treat him as broken, but as a whole person who was not defined by his blindness or scars. Through her love and care, Dan realized that intimacy and companionship was still possible, that his injuries did not preclude a full life of marriage, family, and purpose. Amber—and the love between her and Dan—became a sacramental sign that what is broken can be transformed into something abundant and new.

We can all choose to be part of this moving story of the rising of God's people from suffering to new life. Because we are each a pathway of God's incarnational initiative, not only can we personally be resurrected by the power of the Holy Spirit, we can also participate in the life of God to help others be risen as well. At some point, all of us need to be reminded of who we truly are as a sacred creation of God, to be reminded that God's Spirit will faithfully penetrate even the darkest of places to bring about light, to be reminded that resurrection is not just possible but imminent. God has given us to one another to be companions in the journey of life in God.

***

Even the mightiest of empires cannot prevent God's inbreaking into history to bring about goodness. Through our commitment to the incarnational design of life, we have the great honor of helping God bring an alternate future into reality within us and around us, most especially for those plunged into suffering and anguish. When have you been risen from the ashes to new life? Was the new life what you expected or imagined? What role did others play in your being risen?

+

8 | NAVIGATE

B ecause God is never satisfied with any obstacles we erect between ourselves and God, the Holy Spirit seeks every opportunity to overcome obstructions in order to bless the world with the goodness God intends. One way God overcomes obstruction is by inbreaking along the navigational path: God winds around obstruction by taking alternate routes in order to erupt into time and bring about goodness in the present moment.

God navigates obstruction

During World War II the Nazis killed six million Jews in the most ghastly ways imaginable. With only 21 million Jews across the world at that time, approximately 28% of Jewish people were wiped from the earth in the Holocaust. Operation Reinhard was the largest single murder campaign: in the 21 months from March 1942 to November 1943, the Nazis executed an unfathomable 1.7 million Jews by gas chamber at three death camps: Belzec, Sobibor, and Treblinka. Add to this terror the constant, daily humiliations and sadistic tortures inflicted on this vulnerable people, which included beatings, forced starvation, laboratory experimentation, and death marches in freezing temperatures.

Viktor Frankl found himself trapped in this hell on earth for close to three years. In the shadow of the crematorium, death was constant, faceless, looming. Somehow in this torturous environment, Viktor managed to focus his life on serving others, offering suffering inmates hope and kindness. Instead of turning away from the dying, he would stay by their side, listen to them, provide them comfort, even hold their hands. Though he could not save them, he could witness to their dignity and accompany them with love. At other times, Viktor would give hope to those in despair by reminding them of what was waiting for them outside the prison: children, family, special work projects only they could complete. Viktor gave them a reason to live. "In my distress I called upon the Lord; to my God I cried for help. From his temple he heard my voice, and my cry to him reached his ears" (Psalm 18:6). Viktor spoke about how this service of loving response to his suffering companions gave his own suffering meaning. This is the very heart of God inbreaking into the world to respond to the cries of anguish.

Even in this most ruinous of places, God's Spirit entered through Viktor Frankl to touch those around him. This is a testament to the unstoppability of God's Spirit: not even the military might of the Nazis with their expertly built prisons and cruel, sadistic guards could stop God's inbreaking into the hearts of the people confined within their walls.

Viktor Frankl's story is a striking, humbling, and inspiring guide for all of us, especially those trapped in prisons, brothels, U.S. Immigration and Customs Enforcement (ICE) detention facilities, and any number of places where people are held against their will in appalling conditions that reduce them to objects or machines, thereby causing immense psychological and physical torture and desecrating their inherent human

dignity. God's Spirit is fiercely and relentlessly at every moment seeking to flow into as
many openings as possible to uplift those
who suffer. If God's agile Spirit can find
navigational paths into Nazi death camps,
then God can—and does—find ways to enter
every situation we may face.

Indeed, the birth of Jesus itself is God's
persistent inbreaking along the navigational
path. The Roman Empire was an occupying
force that subjugated the Jews with heavy
taxation and exploitation, corrupt leadership,
and frequent brutality. After all, this is the
Empire that perfected the tool of crucifixion
into a standardized form of execution. In
addition to the Roman Empire, the people
were also subjected to local power structures—state and religious. The Gospel of
Luke captures the many layers of power
across the region: "In the fifteenth year of the
reign of Emperor Tiberius, when Pontius
Pilate was governor of Judea, and Herod was
ruler of Galilee, and his brother Philip ruler
of the region of Ituraea and Trachonitis, and
Lysanias ruler of Abilene, during the high
priesthood of Annas and Caiaphas, the word
of God came" (Luke 3:1-2). *The word of God
came:* even with all these intersecting sources

of power, God penetrated into history. Indeed, even the might of the Roman occupying power was no match for a fourteen-year-old girl who said yes to God and changed human history forever. God is infinitely ingenious and so will surface routes that wind around institutional obstruction, or ferret out any cracks within it, to find self-expression into historical circumstances.

All of us everywhere, no matter our circumstances, can make ourselves available to the navigational inbreaking of God's Holy Spirit to become a source of God's goodness for all in our midst. In this way, our lives are always beyond the grip of institutional control, for no institution—regardless of its might—can prevent us from becoming an incarnational pathway for God's self-expression in the world. God's Spirit ceaselessly roams the earth to discover any and every opening to enter and sow goodness. As God promises us in Isaiah, "[D]o not fear, for I am with you, do not be afraid, for I am your God; I will strengthen you, I will help you, I will uphold you with my victorious right hand" (Isaiah 41:10).

God does not violate

It is very difficult to accept that God permits such abhorrent situations of death like the Holocaust or chattel slavery or the vast, conflict-related famine in Sudan. There is no satisfactory answer to this, and this can be a great struggle to accept, especially during times of tragedy and hardship. What can be said is that one reason God takes the navigational path is because God refuses to violate us. God is love, and love does not force itself upon another, for to violate another is to transgress the very dignity that God has sewn into our being. For God to violate us as a way to teach us not to violate others is a nonsensical hypocrisy that breaches the spiritual principles God chose to govern our life together. Love simply cannot exist without freedom—the freedom to consent.

It is difficult to understand how God can give such a terrifying freedom to humanity, a freedom that, as we see in so many devastating atrocities across time and place, is wielded as a weapon against humanity, against creation, against God's very self. Yet, this is how life is mysteriously designed: God invites and calls and waits, requesting our consent so that our yes can be a true act of love rather than coercion. Love affords the freedom to choose or it is not love at all.

God's valuing of consent as fundamental to participation in God's life is highlighted in the Annunciation (Luke 1:26-38). God does not impose the incarnation upon Mary but invites her to give her consent to God's desires for her life. As such, the birth of Jesus himself hinges on—and is an act of—human freedom. The revelatory importance of this cannot be overstated: the love that is God is not domination but rather a self-giving love that respects the freedom of those with whom God interacts. God does not force God's self upon us, but continually beckons, calls, invites us into a living communion. God does not, will not, violate but waits for our yes.

Not all of us reach yes as quickly as young Mary. For many of us, consent takes time or circumstances or understanding. As a young woman, Dorothy Day was not religious. She was a journalist and a political activist, who at times lived a bohemian lifestyle. She had relationships outside of marriage, an abortion, and later a daughter with the man she loved. When her daughter was born, Dorothy experienced a profound turning point: she felt an overwhelming gratitude for the gift of life and felt deeply moved to raise her child in faith. She started to feel mysteriously drawn to the Catholic Church with its rituals and sacramental life. She chose to baptize her daughter and to be received into the Catholic Church herself, a decision that cost her dearly as it resulted in her partner leaving her. Undeterred, Dorothy continued to follow God's Holy Spirit and founded the Catholic Worker Movement, which grew into a dedicated force for justice and mercy in the 20th century and continues today. God did not erase her past or force her future but met her where she was and patiently waited for her yes. "Listen! I am standing at the door, knocking; if you hear my voice and open the door, I will come in to you and eat with you, and you with me" (Revelation 3:20). God will not force God's way into our lives; God waits for us to open the door.

Navigation produces surprising gifts

God's inbreaking into history along these alternate routes frequently generates incredible gifts that are usually unforeseen, beyond prediction, and out past the reaches of our imagination. Indeed, this is a hallmark of God's navigational inbreaking: astonishing self-expressions that we never could have planned or engineered. "Now to him who by the power at work within us is able to accomplish abundantly far more than all we can ask or imagine" (Ephesians 3:20). God's Spirit enters into the local historical context of institutional obstruction to take what is broken and bring about something beautiful.

One example of this navigational path of inbreaking is blues music. Blues began to erupt into history in the late 1860s through the freed Black American community as a response to the vicious backlash during the Reconstruction and Jim Crow eras. Ruthlessly crucified by white America, God's Holy Spirit wound around the many intensely inhumane barriers imposed upon Black people to find expression as music—to be healing to a hurting people, to give expression to their brilliance, to demand humanity's witness of the intense obstruction of the U.S. government in the life of God. God's Spirit always finds ways through even the harshest of oppression to break into the world to bless it.

God's inbreaking into history to provide unexpected gifts is a consistent pattern of God's response to institutional obstruction. It is all around us: the Barefoot College in India that trains rural villagers—especially women, often grandmothers—to become solar engineers, health workers, artisans, and teachers, even if they are illiterate; the restorative justice circles in Oakland, California, which work to interrupt the school-to-prison pipeline by bringing together students, teachers, and families to address harm and repair relationships rather than rely on punishment and suffering; indeed, this book, which has flowered in response to the Roman Catholic Church's imposition of the stained glass ceiling upon women called to priesthood. Even as God gives us the freedom to reject God, God still faithfully, persistently, and ingeniously finds ways to erupt into history to give of God's very self to uplift the world. "Be astonished! Be astounded! For a work is being done in your days that you would not believe if you were told" (Habakkuk 1:5).

***

Because God is eager to navigate around obstructions to enter time and give us that which is good, we can keep our awareness trained on the promptings of the Spirit and give ourselves over to how God desires to move through us. Through this practice of awareness, we can expand our participation in the life of God, even in the face of institutional obstruction. Where in your life do you experience God's inbreaking along the navigational path? How can you lean into these currents of incarnational flow to expand your participation in the life of God?

+

9 | DISRUPT

In addition to the navigational path, a second way that God's Spirit overcomes institutional obstruction is by inbreaking along the path of disruption. God is intensely working to dismantle every source of crucifixion on earth. Because God does not coerce or violate humanity against our will, the primary way that powerful institutions are brought into alignment with God is through direct challenge to their obstruction.

God overcomes through disruption

Disruption happens when God enters into history along the navigational path and turns this inbreaking directly onto the institution to dismantle the source of the crucifixion and bring it into alignment with God. This is perhaps the most difficult call to participation in the life in God: because the disruptor directly threatens the institution's status quo, the institution responds with swift and brutal crucifixion in an effort to protect itself from the transformative power of the Holy Spirit. Cooperating with the call to disruption requires a willingness to be crucified in order to provide God with an ongoing opening for institutional transformation. This crucifixion can include anything from verbal violence to physical violence and even death.

In this way, there are two crosses. First, there is the cross we are given—that is, the cross foisted upon us due to circumstances beyond our control, such as being born a Black person in the U.S. or a girl under Taliban rule or a person with physical disabilities in a world utterly designed for the able-bodied. Jesus himself was born a Jew into the oppressive occupation of the Roman Empire. These are very difficult crosses to bear in and of themselves, and God responds in these situations by steadily inbreaking along the navigational path to bring us goodness. However, there is a second cross: the cross we consciously and willingly choose on behalf of God, to help God build a world that works for all creation. The second cross is the cross of Christ: to voluntarily work with God to challenge and transform institutional obstruction to bring the institution into alignment with God, whatever the cost. "If any want to become my followers, let them deny themselves and take up their cross and follow me" (Mark 8:34).

We see God's inbreaking along the path of disruption in the extraordinary work of Martin Luther King, Jr. and the many leaders and participants of the Civil Rights movement. Even the savage terror of the Jim Crow south could not prevent God's incarnational initiative from inbreaking into history as this inspired movement for justice. Paying the very heavy price of crucifixion, the Black American community and their allies heroically facilitated the inbreaking of God, which culminated in the Civil Rights Act of 1964 and the Voting Rights Act of 1965. "Is not this the fast that I choose: to loose the bonds of injustice, to undo the thongs of the yoke, to let the oppressed go free, and to break every yoke? Is it not to share your bread with the hungry, and bring the homeless poor into your house; when you see the naked, to cover them, and not to hide yourself from your own kin? Then your light shall break forth like the dawn, and your healing shall spring up quickly; your vindicator shall go before you, the glory of the Lord shall be your rear guard" (Isaiah 58:6-8). Walking the path of disruption is the ultimate sacrifice for God because it places us in harm's way to make real God's project of salvation on earth.

The path of disruption flows from a deep love for God and God's people, even for the institution itself. The disruptor criticizes the institution from a place of love to force the institution to gaze into the abyss of darkness and acknowledge its outright betrayal of God. Thus, while our call to the path of disruption may be inspired by or flow from personal experience, its work is not aimed at personal gain but is undertaken on behalf of the crucified community that suffers at the hands of institutional obstruction. While charity is God's inbreaking along the navigational path, justice work and community organizing are God's inbreaking along the path of disruption because they seek to end the source of crucifixion by bringing it into alignment with God.

Discerning the source of disruption

Of course, not all disruption comes from God. How can we tell which disruption is coming from God and which is coming from something else, like culture or fear or hatred? One way to discern whether any particular disruption is coming from God is to trace it to its ends: that is, to evaluate the fruit of the disruption—its impact and outcome. "The fruit of the light is found in all that is good and right and true" (Ephesians 5:9); and "the fruit of the Spirit is love, joy, peace, patience, kindness, generosity, faithfulness, gentleness, and self-control" (Galatians 5:22-23). Disruption that is the inbreaking of God into historical circumstances is rooted in sacrifice for the other and, therefore, expands, includes, and uplifts; forgives, heals, and reconciles; brings about freedom and flourishing. In other words, movements of disruption that are of God make salvation real in the present moment.

On the other hand, disruption that comes from the world is rooted in serving the self and, therefore, excludes and subjugates; sows hatred and alienation; exploits, demeans, and dismisses; benefits the few at the expense of the many; shrinks human decency and undermines the fulfillment of goodness. In other words, movements of disruption that come from the world create crucified victims. Disruption of this type cannot come from God because it betrays the very spiritual principles that God chose to govern life on earth. "Every good tree bears good fruit, but the bad tree bears bad fruit. A good tree cannot bear bad fruit, nor can a bad tree bear good fruit. Every tree that does not bear good fruit is cut down and thrown into the fire. Thus you will know them by their fruits" (Matthew 7:17-20). As the life and death of Jesus reveal, God does not sacrifice others for the sake of God's self, but rather God sacrifices God's self for the sake of others. Put simply, God does not crucify; God is crucified.

Consider the fruit of the following two events. In 1943, Gonzalo and Felicitas Méndez tried to enroll their three young children in the neighborhood school in Westminster, California, but were told the kids must attend the "Mexican school," a run-down building with fewer resources and lower expectations for students. Outraged, Gonzalo organized other families to bring a lawsuit on behalf of all Mexican-American children affected by school segregation. In 1946, the District Court ruled in favor of the Méndez family, stating that segregating Mexican-American children was unconstitutional, a decision upheld the next year by the U.S. Court of Appeals for the Ninth Circuit. The ruling ended school segregation in California and set a crucial precedent for the famous *Brown v. Board of Education* decision of the Supreme Court, which made school segregation illegal across the nation. "He has told you, O mortal, what is good; and what does the Lord require of you but to do justice, and to love kindness, and to walk humbly with your God" (Micah 6:8).

Now contemplate the fruit of this event: in 2013, the U.S. Supreme Court ruled that a key provision of the Voting Rights Act of 1965 was unconstitutional, effectively dismantling one of the law's most powerful protections against racial discrimination in voting. By a 5-4 decision, the Court under Chief Justice John Roberts struck down the requirement for states and localities with a history of voter suppression to seek federal approval (preclearance) before changing their voting laws. As a direct result of the ruling, some states rushed to enact restrictive voting measures such as stricter voter ID laws, ballot access restrictions, polling place closures, and heavily gerrymandered redistricting plans. "They have neither knowledge nor understanding, they walk around in darkness; all the foundations of the earth are shaken" (Psalm 82:5). These steps are intentionally aimed at diluting the voting power of minority voters, undermining the very goodness of God for which Martin Luther King, Jr. and the civil rights movement sacrificed.

When we trace these two events to their conclusions and evaluate their fruit through the lens of God's project of salvation on earth, we can see that the first event liberates the oppressed to bring about flourishing, while the second event creates crucified victims. Disruption that is the inbreaking of God into history is always aimed at creating a life together that works for all. When we consent and cooperate with God's Spirit, the fruit of our lives and our work is the goodness that uplifts the world.

Overcoming as prophetic

These two paths of the resurrection principle, navigational and disruption, are prophetic—that is, destabilizing to that which is out of alignment with God—but in different ways. First, the inbreaking of God along the navigational path is prophetic because it challenges the institution by its very existence, laying bare the false or flawed claims of the institution about that particular reality. We see this prophetic nature in the LGBTQ community, particularly in the nonbinary and trans communities, whose very existence destabilizes the long-held, entrenched gender ideology that assigns roles, traits, and expectations according to biological difference, an approach known as biological determinism.

Inside this ideology of the gender binary, men are expected to be strong, rational, authoritative, decisive, and protective—thought to be designed by God to hold positions of authority in the public sphere and over the family. Women, on the other hand, are expected to be nurturing, emotional, dependent, gentle, obedient, modest, and self-sacrificing—thought to be designed by God to be naturally designed for subservience to men and the work of the domestic sphere.

These categories are so heavily policed across religion and broader society that parents of healthy babies born intersex—with chromosomes, sex organs, and/or genitalia of both biological sexes—are frequently pressured into medically unnecessary surgery with the presupposition that their children's lives will be better if they fit into a predetermined gender category. Rather than allowing these bodies to simply exist as they are—healthy but unique forms in the infinite unfolding of expression of human bodies—intersex infants and young children are put through irreversible surgeries that can cause long-lasting psychological harm and permanent biological damage, including difficulties conceiving children and the impairment of sexual sensation and function—a very steep price to pay to make an unusual yet perfectly healthy physical form fit into a preconceived notion of gender. "For my thoughts are not your thoughts, nor are your ways my ways, says the Lord. For as the heavens are higher than the earth, so are my ways higher than your ways and my thoughts than your thoughts" (Isaiah 55:8-9).

While gender nonconforming people have existed down through time and across many cultures (for example, the central Rabbinic text of Judaism known as the Talmud cites seven different genders, and many Indigenous nations have recognized Two-Spirit people), in today's world the force of the gender binary carries with it an unyielding momentum. However, if we simply use our faculties to observe the reality around us, we see that even on its surface, the gender binary does not accurately reflect the human person but is a narrowing of possibility that obstructs our ability to truly understand ourselves as humans. Indeed, if we are honest, how many of us fit into such neat and clean categories? We all know women who are strong leaders and men who are emotional. Even with intense policing of categories across religion and society, gender expression simply cannot be fully restrained.

This is precisely why the nonbinary community is considered threatening: their presence lays bare the truth that the vast majority of people—if not all—are nonbinary in the sense that we all have a fascinating blend of traits from both the masculine and feminine categories, along with many other attributes that have not yet been assigned to gender, like being playful, lazy, adaptable, resourceful, wise, imaginative, or resilient. We also inherit traits from ethnic culture and family upbringing, not to mention any number of strange quirks we develop, like talking to our plants, making strange faces while we think, or the penchant to collect odd items. In addition, our traits—whatever they are—can evolve with time as we experience life and grow as a person.

In this way, the existence of the nonbinary community makes us face ourselves: that things are other than proclaimed, that there is a richer understanding of gender to be embraced if we are to better understand humanity as a whole. Rather than welcoming this prophetic challenge to our current theories of the human person—and allowing the challenge to set us free from error—the nonbinary community is demonized as deviant in order to preserve and propagate the illusion of the present social order. "More in number than the hairs of my head are those who hate me without cause; many are those who would destroy me, my enemies who accuse me falsely" (Psalm 69:4).

Similarly, the trans community is prophetic simply by virtue of its existence. For example, the Roman Catholic Church teaches that the human person is a unity of body and soul, where the spiritual and physical dimensions of a person are not separate or opposed but form a single, integrated reality that constitutes the fullness of the human person. Another way to put this is that we, as a unified creation, have and reveal a particular share in the life of God. This is a beautiful theology that seems to describe the vast majority of people. However, science and the voices of the trans community are pointing to a new horizon of insight that is dawning: there is a small percentage of people for whom this is not the case, for whom the body and soul are not a unity.

Similar to intersex people, trans people are a unique expression of the infinite unfolding of human expression down through time. As such, they present humanity with the opportunity to learn. Because trans people—like all people—have a share in the life of God, their presence is revealing something about who God is. For example, the God who animates all creation is the God of evolution. Indeed, evolution is an essential aspect of the natural world. Perhaps God is incarnating this particular characteristic of God's self within the trans community, uplifting them a sacramental sign of God's inclination to evolve into new forms.

However, instead of allowing the trans community to lead humanity to a more complex understanding of the human person in God, they are demonized in order to shield institutions from the uncomfortable dislocation of the Holy Spirit, who continues to prod us into seeing that there is always more to life than what meets the eye, always more illusion and misconception to let go, always more insight to embrace. "Do not be conformed to this world, but be transformed by the renewing of your minds, so that you may discern what is the will of God—what is good and acceptable and perfect" (Romans 12:2).

While the inbreaking of God along the navigational path is prophetic simply by virtue of its existence, the inbreaking of God along the path of disruption is prophetic because it aims to remove the source of crucifixion. Such disruption requires the ministry of truthtelling to liberate all those caught in the obstruction's clutches. Where the navigational path evidences God's creative self-expression into history, which challenges narrow definitions or understand-ings of reality, the path of disruption—as seen so clearly in the life of Martin Luther King, Jr.—is intent on bringing the institutional obstruction into alignment with God so that the crucifixion ends. Both paths are integral to making real God's project of goodness on earth.

The inbreaking of God's Holy Spirit into history is rarely welcomed in the present moment precisely because it unsettles, cajoles, destabilizes, and challenges the status quo in ways that often provoke resistance or fear. Again and again, what is of God first appears scandalous, threatening, or even heretical because it exposes everything from the limitations of how reality has been defined to the outright hostility to goodness that demands conversion of heart. "I am about to do a new thing; now it springs forth, do you not perceive it" (Isaiah 43:19).

Scripture captures this human tendency to demonize and persecute the disruptive inbreaking of God. The prophets are mocked and persecuted (Jeremiah 38:4-6; 2 Chronicles 36:15-16; Amos 7:10-15); Jesus is accused of blasphemy and executed as a criminal (Matthew 26:47-27:66; Mark 14:43-15:47; Luke 22:47-23:56; John 18:1-19:42); St. Paul is derided as an agitator, imprisoned, and constantly facing violence (Acts 9:23-25; Acts 14:19-20; Acts 21:30-31). Only with the passage of time and rising of insight is God's inbreaking into history identified for what it truly is: the unfolding of a new creation that brings us that much closer to God's dream of fullness of life. This is a puzzling reality of the Spirit's entrance into materiality: its authenticity is often only recognized in retrospect when the fruit of God's goodness—love, mercy, peace, justice, and new life—can no longer be denied. What will it take for us as a human family to collectively recognize the inbreaking of the living God into the present moment?

***

All of us have a place within where the wellspring of God's Spirit flows beyond the grip of institutional control. By following God's incarnational initiative at work within us, we can sharpen our spiritual senses to identify the path of becoming that will lead us to greater participation in the life of God. The more we participate in the life of God, the more freedom and fulfillment and meaning we experience, and the more fully we blossom into who we are to bless the world. It is to this untouched place where God dwells within us that we now turn, so that God can lead us beyond institutional obstruction into fullness of life.

+

PART FOUR:
SPIRITUAL EXERCISES

"In the silence of the heart God speaks.
If you face God in prayer and silence,
God will speak to you.
Then you will know that you are nothing.
It is only when you realize your nothingness,
your emptiness, that God can fill you with
God's self."

—Mother Teresa

Engaging with Part Four

Now that you are familiar with God's incarnational initiative and the spiritual principles that govern our life together on earth, Part Four leads you through ten spiritual exercises that provide God an opportunity to bestow insight into how these principles are at work in your own life. Chapter 10 offers the first three exercises, which focus on how God desires to incarnate in your life and whether institutions are obstructing God's desires. Chapter 11 provides the second three exercises, which help you contemplate God's inbreaking along the navigational path and how you might expand your participation in these incarnational bright spots. Chapter 12 provides Exercises 7 to 9, which lead you in a reflection on God's inbreaking along the path of disruption. Chapter 13 provides the final contemplation, which gives you the opportunity to sort through all the movements of your prayer so that you can make a discernment about the path forward.

Blessings upon your journey.

10 | CLARIFY

T hese ten spiritual exercises in Part Four direct your prayer and reflection into how you can follow God's incarnational initiative onto the path of becoming, even in the face of powerful institutional obstruction in the life of God. Before embarking on your journey of prayer, carefully read the overview and general instructions below.

Overview

There are ten spiritual exercises spread over four chapters. The first three exercises guide you through reflections that clarify whether and how institutional obstruction is at work in your life. The second three exercises help you identify areas of God's inbreaking along the navigational path into your life and invite you to reflect on how you might expand your participation in these areas of incarnational flow. Exercises 7 to 9 help you investigate whether God is inviting you onto the path of disruption to directly challenge the institutional obstruction causing the crucifixion in your life. The final exercise guides you into a deep reflection upon the various possibilities that surface throughout the exercises so that you can discern the invitation forward from God. The hope is that at the completion of the exercises you will see the path of fullness of life that lies beyond the grip of institutional control so that you can more fully become who you are to bless the world.

General Instructions

When entering into these spiritual exercises, do your best to remove distraction, invite quiet, and cultivate the inner stillness you need to go deep into prayer and reflection. Resist any temptation to rush or do the exercises in a surface way, but instead afford these pages and God the time and space that is truly needed for your path with God to come into view.

If you think it will be helpful, before you start, take a quick, surface look through all ten exercises to get a sense of their flow.

When you are ready, begin Exercise 1. Each exercise builds upon the previous, so it is important to do each one to clarity before proceeding to the next. You may need to pray through a particular exercise more than once to receive clarity—a common occurrence when doing deep reflection and prayer. If you get stuck on an exercise, consider having a conversation with someone like a close friend or spiritual director to uncover the source of the difficulty. There is no need to feel anxiety: if you stick with the inquiry into your life, eventually things will become clear in the light of the Holy Spirit. Just accept the unfolding as it happens and be at peace.

While the order of exercises is set, you are encouraged to find ways of entering into them that work best for you. For example, if music aids in your connection with God, incorporate it into your reflection time. If discussion helps you process your experience, invite a trustworthy companion or small group to complete these exercises with you. If writing helps you receive insight, keep a journal. Before you begin, ask the Holy Spirit to guide you in creating an environment and practice of prayer that helps facilitate deep connection with God.

When you begin an exercise, read it prayerfully all the way through to get a sense of where it goes, and then return to the beginning and delve deeply into each prompt. When you reach a point of clarity for each question, write down any insights you receive. Perhaps purchase a notebook to use exclusively for these exercises. Your written reflections will be greatly beneficial as you progress through the reflections, as well as into future weeks and months as you live out your path.

Finally, trust that God will show up. Remember, God deeply desires to be known by you, to build a dynamic and intimate love relationship with you. Through these exercises you are inviting this type of authentic encounter with the living God. It is God's pleasure to dwell with you and enjoy with you the heartfelt communion that is the love you share.

Exercise 1: Contemplate your life

These first three exercises help you gain clarity into how God is incarnating in your life and whether institutional obstruction is impacting your participation in the life of God. This exercise guides you in an initial contemplation of how God is expressing God's self in and through your life. If desired, revisit the concepts in Part One, then consider these questions:

- What is your life for? What goodness of God do you feel moved to bring into the world?
- Who is your life for? Who is blessed by your share in the life of God?
- What actions do you take to make this goodness of God a reality in the world? Be specific.

This exercise may bring movements of deep emotion, wonder, and joy. Its content is a reminder that God has given you as a gift to creation, as well as to God's own self. Your life matters infinitely to God and to the world: no other being can bless the world with your unique share in the life of God. You are irreplaceable. Dwell on any insights you receive, allowing them to sink into the depth of your being. Proceed when you feel rooted in the wonderful mystery of your life in God.

Exercise 2: Name the obstruction

This exercise helps you identify whether and how institutions may be obstructing the full expression of your share in the life of God. If desired, revisit the concepts in Chapters 4 and 5, then consider these questions:

- Reflect on your answers to Exercise 1. Do you experience institutional barriers to fully expressing your share in the life of God? Name the barriers and identify their source.
- What specific techniques is the institution using to obstruct your participation in the life of God? Be specific.
- What symptoms of institutional obstruction are showing up in your life? Consider everyday life as well as the full arc of your journey.

This exercise may surface movements of anger, sadness, or despair. Allow them to rise up, acknowledge them, and then temporarily set them aside until the next exercise. As much as you are able, gaze upon the dynamics at play in your life from a place of curiosity and freedom, as if you are an external observer interested in gaining insight into the specific working parts of the situation.

NOTE: While this exercise focuses on institutional obstruction, you may discover other sources of obstruction, like your own past decisions or family interference. If this is the case, simply be honest with yourself and with God about what you see. Pray, reflect, and address these other sources of interference accordingly. If helpful, speak to a spiritual director to sort through your insights.

Exercise 3: Identify the cost

This exercise prompts an exploration of the cost you pay as a result of the institutional obstruction in your life. This can be a deeply painful reflection. Allow yourself and God the time and space needed to contemplate these questions:

- Sort through your insights from Exercise 2. What suffering do you experience at the hands of institutional obstruction? Be specific.

- What goodness of God has been prevented from entering into everyday life because of the obstruction? Consider the cost to you, to humanity and creation, to God. Be specific and thorough.

- What emotions are you experiencing as you contemplate this loss? Name them. When you are clear on what you are feeling, bring these movements before God and allow God to minister to you.

This exercise may surface movements of anger, surprise, frustration, disappointment, or despair. Allow these movements to fully arise without judgment. You are entitled to your feelings. Contemplate whether the emotions you feel are not just your own emotions but God incarnating within you—a touchpoint of unity. Resist the temptation to rush through this reflection. If helpful, take several breaths and ask the Holy Spirit to give you the grace to dwell in this painful place. Give God the time and space God needs to teach you about the dynamics at play in your life.

***

Through these initial exercises you have hopefully received a picture of how God desires to incarnate in and through you, whether and how institutions are obstructing this incarnational expression, and, if so, the cost of this interference. With this initial clarity, the next step is to more fully explore the bright spots of God's incarnational expression in your life, and to consider how you can lean into them to expand your participation in the life of God for the good of the world.

+

11 | EXPAND

These next three exercises direct your prayer into how God is navigating around the institutional obstruction in your life to find self-expression. The purpose of these reflections is to help you see how you can expand your participation in the life of God to create an alternate future of joy and flourishing beyond the grip of institution control.

Exercise 4: Examine incarnational flow

This exercise builds on Exercise 1 to gain deeper insight into how God's incarnational initiative is at work in your life. Review the insights you received from Exercise 1, then consider these questions:

- Where in your life are you able to fully express your share in the life of God to bless the world with goodness? Be specific.

- How can you expand or increase your participation in these areas? Be specific.

- Do you see any new areas of opportunity for facilitating the inbreaking of God's goodness into the world? Be specific.

As you contemplate these questions, be open to any inspiration that may arise. Let insights float up without censorship or judgment. This exercise may evoke movements of joy, inspiration, excitement, gratitude, or a sense of honor in response to such splendid invitations to participation in the life of God. Dwell on any insights, pondering them in your heart.

Exercise 5: Envision an alternate future

This exercise invites you to envision the alternate future brought about by your expanded participation in the life of God. This is a contemplation that uses the eye of hope to glimpse what is possible in God. Consider these questions:

- Reflect on the insights from Exercise 4. Which possibilities do you feel genuinely moved to embrace? Search your heart honestly in the light of the Holy Spirit.

- Imagine yourself living out these possibilities. Use all five senses to bring this alternate future to life. How will your life be blessed? How will others' lives be blessed? What sense of meaning and purpose will this path give you? Explore.

- How will living out this alternate future change your experience of crucifixion? How will this new life impact your relationship with the obstructing institution? Be specific.

The alternate future that emerges in your reflections has great significance: it is a share of God's project of salvation that is made real in everyday life through your companionship with God. Allow its meaning to sink into the depth of your being. This exercise may evoke movements of joy, excitement, humility, and awe at the goodness of this invitation from the living God. Emerge from this exercise with insight into the inbreaking of God along the navigational path, which winds around institutional obstruction to bring you to a life of joy and meaning through greater participation in the life of God.

Exercise 6: Engineer your life

Now that you have sorted through what is possible and unearthed an alternate future in God, reflect upon what it would take to engineer your life so that this path becomes the center of your life. Consider these questions:

- What do you need to let go, be pruned of, or sacrifice to bring this alternate future into reality? Consider both interior needs and external factors.

- What supports do you need to bring this alternate future into being? Consider the inner graces you need from God as well as outer supports like resources and community. Are these supports in place? If not, what would it take to put them in place?

- Sit at length with this vision of new life. What would it take for you to say yes to this alternate future? Be honest with yourself and with God.

This exercise may produce a variety of movements from excitement, joy, and inspiration to anxiety, doubt, fear, and false humility. Stay with the exercise until the movements settle and the invitation from God becomes clear. Movements from God create a deep sense of peace and rightness, even if the path is difficult and fraught with challenge. Such peace emanates from a deep knowing of God's goodness and fidelity— from the visceral understanding that we belong to God and that God is always with us. The settling of the movements may take some days of prayer, discussion with companions, or a session with a trained spiritual director. Trust yourself to recognize God's communication, and allow for the time and space that is needed for this communication to unfold. Clarity will come.

***

The exercises in this chapter hopefully helped you gain insight into the inbreaking of God into your life along the navigational path— how God's Spirit is already winding around, or wanting to wind around, the institutional obstruction in your life to find expression into the world to bring about goodness. The next step is to explore whether God wants to bend your share of God's life back onto the institution to help bring it into alignment with God's project of salvation in everyday life.

+

12 | CHALLENGE

Institutions that obstruct God's incarnational initiative can only be brought into alignment with God by direct challenge. As the life of Jesus reveals, the path of disruption requires the willingness to be crucified—to intentionally place oneself in harm's way on behalf of God. This harm can range from verbal violence to physical violence, even death. These spiritual exercises guide you through a reflection on what the path of disruption might look like for you at this particular time and place in your life, and whether you feel moved by God to pick up this cross.

Exercise 7: Explore possibilities of disruption

The first step when considering the path of disruption is to explore possible ways you can directly challenge the institution. Consider these questions:

- Contemplate the insights from Exercises 4 and 5. Do any of these possibilities from your reflection on the navigational path already directly challenge the institution? If not, are there ways to bend them back onto the institution? Investigate. Be specific.

- Revisit your reflections from Exercise 2. Considering the obstructionist techniques used by the institution, do you see any additional opportunities for direct challenge? Be specific.

- Contemplate all of the possibilities that you unearthed. Which do you feel genuinely moved to embrace? Search your heart in the light of the Holy Spirit. Be honest with yourself and God.

This exercise may surface movements of inspiration, excitement, hope, fear, or anxiety. Allow any movements to float up from a place of freedom. If you feel fear, acknowledge its presence without judgment, then set it aside for the time being and continue the exercise. Notice which movements open up new levels of meaning and purpose for your life. Ponder these reflections deep in your heart.

Exercise 8: Consider the cost

This exercise helps reveal the particular details of your cross: what the costs of crucifixion may be and how they may unfold in everyday life.

- How might you be crucified for following the path of disruption? What are you risking? Be specific.
- What sacrifices are necessary if you are to willingly accept this cost? Be thorough.
- What supports do you need to be able to sustain such a path? Consider the inner graces you need and the outer supports like resources and community. Are these supports in place? If not, what would it take to put them in place?

This exercise may produce movements of fear. Do not allow this fear to tempt you into rushing through the exercise. It is essential to go deep and allow the picture of suffering to emerge. If fear surfaces, allow yourself to feel it without judgment. This is a perfectly natural response when contemplating an invitation to challenge a powerful institution that does harm to humanity and creation. Bring your emotions before Christ hanging on the cross. Allow him the opportunity to speak to you about your fears. Let the picture of your particular cross sink into the depth of your being.

Exercise 9: Ponder the blessings

While there is suffering on the path of disruption, there are also rich and abundant blessings. Consider these questions:

- What blessings might you experience along this specific path of disruption? Are these blessings unique to this path alone?
- How will the world be blessed by your sacrifice? What goodness will enter and who will be uplifted by it?
- How will walking the path of disruption impact your relationship with God? Be specific.

This exercise may produce movements of joy, excitement, profound humility, or unworthiness as you become present to the blessings of the cross. Dwell on these insights. Give God the opportunity to comment on the movements you are experiencing. Linger on the possibilities of this path. Once you receive some clarity on the life that is possible with God, create some space before moving on to the final exercise. Take some time, perhaps a day or more, to allow any additional insights to unfold or percolate. Give yourself time to simply sit with all that has arisen.

***

The exercises in this chapter hopefully helped you discover the possibilities of God's inbreaking into your life along the path of disruption—how God may desire to incarnate through you as direct challenge to the institution in order to bring its crucifixion to an end. The final step of these exercises is to sort through all the movements of your reflections to make a discernment of the path forward in God.

+

13 | DISCERN

You have reached the final contemplation. The first three exercises gave you initial insight into how God is and wants to incarnate in your life, whether and how institutions are obstructing your full participation in the life of God, and the cost the world pays because of this obstruction. The second three exercises uncovered the navigational path that God takes to wind around the institutional obstruction in your life to erupt into history. The last three exercises offered insight into God's inbreaking along the path of disruption—what your chosen cross may look like, as well as its costs and blessings. It is now time to discern the invitation from God for this particular time and place in your life.

Exercise 10: Final contemplation

This final contemplation helps you sort through the range of possibilities that surfaced in your prayer throughout these spiritual exercises. It is important to note that this exercise is not designed as an either/or choice between the navigational path or the path of disruption. You may be entirely moved to one path or the other, but it is also possible—even probable—to discover a third way that blends elements of both paths. The important thing is to bring the full picture of your reflections back into your prayer to allow God's Spirit the opportunity to freely communicate with you about what has arisen. Consider these questions:

- What possibilities of the navigational path most attract you? Which most repel you? Why? Deeply investigate in the light of the Holy Spirit. Be honest about what you see and how you feel regarding each possibility.

- What possibilities of the path of disruption most attract you? Which most repel you? Why? Deeply investigate in the light of the Holy Spirit. Be honest about what you see and how you feel regarding each possibility.

- Considering these various possibilities, which do you feel genuinely moved to embrace? Search your heart in the light of the Holy Spirit. Be completely honest with yourself and with God.

This final contemplation may produce unexpected movements of excitement, fear, joy, or anxiety. Allow all of them to surface without judgment and give them time to settle. It is critical that you be honest with yourself and with God. You have absolutely nothing to prove to anyone, least of all God. You do not need to earn God's love or acceptance: this is already freely and fully given to you by virtue of your humanity. Instead, this exercise is about discovering the invitation from the living God to the path of your becoming for your own well being and the well being of the world. You need only a pure and open heart to receive God's communication and respond to it.

Make an election

When you arrive at a sense of clarity about the path forward, refrain from taking action. Instead, make an election: decide on the path forward, then sit with this decision for one or two days—or longer if need be. As your discernment sinks in, pay very close attention to the movements that surface in response to your decision. Do you feel a sense of rightness and peace that you have chosen well? If not, return to the beginning of this final exercise.

The key grace you are looking for is a deep sense of peace and rightness about the path forward. The physiological sensations that create a feeling of peace and rightness in your body and spirit are God's Spirit incarnating within you to confirm that you have, indeed, recognized and understood God's invitation to the path of becoming beyond the grip of institutional control. When you reach this clarity of peace and a sense of rightness, carve out the time to give sincere thanks to God. Do not rush through this: this gratitude encounter with God is the most important aspect of these exercises and this book. Give the experience of thanking

God its proper due. After you rejoice together, make the formal decision to proceed down the path that has been illuminated for you by God's Holy Spirit. Then, take your first steps.

***

You have uncovered the path of your becoming in God beyond the grip of institutional control. God will be with you at every moment to pour out the grace you need to follow. With each step, bring any decisions into the light of the Holy Spirit. Use a prayer cycle: pray about how to move forward; make the decision from your prayer; live out your decision according to your prayer; then bring the experience and outcome of your decision back into your prayer once again. The living God is your steadfast companion always and will give you the grace you need to become who you are. May you be bold in your petitions, brave in your fidelity, and joyous in living out of your share in the life of God—given for the good of the world.

✝

Take, Lord, and receive all my liberty,
my memory, my understanding,
and my entire will,
all I have and call my own.
You have given all to me.
To you, Lord, I return it.
Everything is yours; do with it what you will.
Give me only your love and your grace;
that is enough for me.

—St. Ignatius of Loyola

CODA

E ach of us has a share in the life of God with which we are invited to bless the world. When we truly grasp the incarnational design of life, our way of seeing is transformed: all life is a miracle, a mystery, a gift pulsing with the perplexing and glorious presence of God. Our hearts become seized by reverence, humbled before the splendor and goodness of it all. The more we encounter God's presence incarnating within and around us, the more willing and able we become to let go of what binds us so that we can embrace God's dream of a world that works for all. We have all been invited into this journey of a lifetime.

While institutions do great damage by obstructing God's inbreaking into our lives, they ultimately hold no final power over God: God's Spirit will always find alternate paths of expression to erupt into the world to bless it, renew it, reconcile it. This is God's eternal promise to us all, freely given and never rescinded. When we feel tempted to despair, let us remember to grow still and turn to the Shepherd Within—that inner place where the wellspring of the incarnation flows. God dwells there always, waiting patiently to guide us onto the path of overcoming that uplifts the world.

+

AFTERWORD

I t is not a given that institutions obstruct God's incarnational initiative. There are many instances where institutions facilitate the inbreaking of God to bring about salvation in the present moment. We see God enter when governments ensure health care, education, clean water, and worker protections; when schools offer space for intellectual exploration and discovery to every student regardless of background; when nonprofits and churches provide experiences of welcoming and loving community; when a country comes together to celebrate the great gift of its unique heritage. There are many ways institutions cooperate with God to make life good.

While this is true, it is also true that far too often institutions are working directly against God, betraying God's vision for a life of goodness together. Such obstruction is laid bare in the creation of crucified victims. When we gaze into the contorted faces of peoples being bombed; of families packed onto boats to risk death in search of a better life; of young women and girls imprisoned in sexual slavery; of people without homes forced to sleep outside in the cold; of those exhausted from working three jobs to put food on the table; of animals made insane by the unspeakable cruelty of factory farms and laboratories—when we look into the eyes of the crucified, we are gazing not only upon their anguish, but on the very anguish of the living God, who cries out from abuse at the hands of God's own creation.

When we contemplate life through this incarnational lens, it becomes rather clear which institutions are in alignment with God and which are not. While those directly affected by the institutional obstruction by far pay the heaviest price, the entire human family—and all creation—also suffers. In fact, we have reached the perilous point in history where humanity is both so technologically advanced, yet so far out of alignment with God, that we are impacting the earth itself, threatening not only our own survival but that of all life on earth.

The Good News is that we can turn things around at any time. All we must do is recognize the incarnational impulse coursing through creation and then design our institutions to facilitate it. While this book explores how individuals can thrive despite institutional obstruction, what is truly needed for God's dream of flourishing to be made real in everyday life is the swift and total reform of any and all institutions that are obstructing the inbreaking of God.

The most effective way to usher in such a transformation is to go to the margins—the crucified—and center their voices and experience. Indeed, the crucified are the only ones who can save us because it is through them that God cries out to urgently alert us to the fundamental misalignment of the institution with God's vision of salvation in the present moment. When the experience and voices of the crucified are taken seriously, they lead us to reorganize institutions and life in ways that honor the hidden spiritual principles that govern life according to God's design. When the institution is brought into alignment with God, crucifixion naturally ceases and the marginalized are welcomed into the center to flourish as God intends.

We must take a moment to let this vision of the full participation of all God's people and what this means sink in: when crucified peoples are able to live as God intends—to fully bless the world with their share in the life of God—this will unleash a tide of goodness that transforms and uplifts all creation far beyond anything we can imagine. In this way, those on the margins point the way to the world of flourishing that works for all. In other words, it is not the powerful who hold the answers, but the marginalized: the crucified are our true leaders. It is the role of the powerful to serve the marginalized, to create the opening for their voices and experiences to be heard so that they can lead us to the new life that God intends. This is the moral obligation of all leadership everywhere.

However, if humanity continues to ignore the spiritual principles that govern life—shaping institutions to produce crucified victims and organizing life in ways that prevent the full participation of all creation in the life of God according to God's desires—then there will be blistering devastation that harms us all. Indeed, if we do not change our ways soon, we will destroy not only humanity, but creation itself.

It is not too late. God is faithfully waiting for us: all we need to do is cooperate. The choice is up to us.

✝

Learn more

Explore the resources listed below to learn more about the stories and issues in this book. This is not a comprehensive list, but a place to start.

SPIRITUAL DIRECTION

> Spiritual Directors International. *SDI – The Home of Spiritual Direction and Companionship.* https://www.sdicompanions.org/ Accessed 18 September 2025.

> Ignatian Spirituality. *Spiritual Direction.* https://www.ignatianspirituality.com/making-good-decisions/spiritual-direction/ Accessed 18 September 2025.

CHAPTER ONE

Tina Crawford and Jy'Aire Smith-Pennick
> Lake, T. (2025, February 22). *When her son was murdered, she wanted revenge. It didn't go as planned.* CNN. https://www.cnn.com/interactive/2025/02/us/tina-crawford-son-murder-delaware-cec-cnnphotos/

Scott Harrison
    Charity: Water. *Scott Harrison's Story.*
    https://www.charitywater.org/about/scott-
    harrison-story Accessed 20 September 2025

charity: water
    Charity: Water. https://www.charity
    water.org/ Accessed 8 September 2025.

Rosa Parks
    The Martin Luther King, Jr. Research and
    Education Institute. *Parks, Rosa.* https://
    kinginstitute.stanford.edu/parks-rosa
    Accessed 8 September 2025.

Bishop Desmond Tutu
    Baker, Aryn. (2021, December 26). *Desmond
    Tutu, Anti-Apartheid Campaigner Who Tried
    to Heal the World, Dies at 90.* Time. https://
    time.com/6131611/desmond-tutu-dies-
    south-africa/

CHAPTER 2

Simone Biles
    Olympics. *Simone Biles: A Journey from Early
    Years to Sporting Glory.* https://
    www.olympics.com/en/athletes/simone-biles
    Accessed 8 September 2025.

Amanda Gorman
   Gorman, Amanda. *Wordsmith. Change-maker.* https://www.theamandagorman.com/ Accessed 8 September 2025.

Milo Runkle
   Mercy For Animals. (2017, September 7). *Founder Milo Runkle Opens up About His First Open Rescues* [Video]. YouTube. https://www.youtube.com/watch?v=_EAd2XBYIms

Factory farming

   Mercy For Animals. https://mercyforanimals. org/ Accessed 8 September 2025.

   Compassion in World Farming. https://www.ciwf.com/ Accessed 8 September 2025.

Food waste

   ReFED: Rethink Food Waste. https://refed.org/food-waste/consumer-food-waste Accessed 8 September 2025.

   Feeding America: Our Work. https://www.feedingamerica.org/our-work/reduce-food-waste Accessed 8 September 2025.

Angelita Castro Kelly

Filipina Women's Network. (2015, June 15). *In Memoriam: Dr. Angelita Castro-Kelly, U.S. FWN100™ '07, NASA'S Fearless Filipina Diplomat.* https://filipinawomensnetwork.org/epahayagan/dr-angelita-castro-kelly-us-fwn100-07-passes

Isaac T. Hopper

E.M.N. (2023). *Isaac Tatem Hopper*. EBSCO Research. https://www.ebsco.com/research-starters/biography/isaac-tatem-hopper Accessed 8 September 2025.

Sr. Helen Prejean

Ministry Against the Death Penalty. *Sister Helen Prejean.* https://www.sisterhelen.org/ Accessed 8 September 2025.

Sandy Hook Promise

Sandy Hook Promise. *Preventing Gun Violence.* https://www.sandyhookpromise.org/ Accessed 8 September 2025

Oskar Schindler

Holocaust Encyclopedia. *Oskar Schindler.* https://encyclopedia.ushmm.org/content/en/article/oskar-schindler Accessed 8 September 2025.

Harvey Weinstein
    Dwyer, C. and Gomez Sarmiento, I. (2025,
    July 1). *The cases against Harvey Weinstein: A
    timeline of allegations and trials.* NPR. https://
    www.npr.org/2025/04/20/nx-s1-5075185/
    harvey-weinstein-allegations-trials-timeline

Bill Cosby
    Alter, C. (2014, November 24). *Everything
    You Need to Know About the Bill Cosby
    Scandal.* Time. https://time.com/3602131/
    bill-cosby-sexual-assault-allegations-guide/

Bernie Madoff
    FBI. *Bernie Madoff Case.* https://
    www.fbi.gov/history/famous-cases/bernie-
    madoff Accessed 8 September 2025.

Gary Thynes and the dog
    Gunderson, K. (2025, July 30). *Dog hailed as
    hero after leading stranger to 2 unresponsive
    people at tent encampment along the North
    Shore.* WTAE-TV.
    https://www.wtae.com/article/dog-stranger-
    aid-two-unresponsive-people-pittsburghs-
    north-shore/65556132

Matt Swatzell and Erik Fitzgerald
    Blackshere, R. (2024, February 3). *Widower
    forges friendship with man in crash that killed
    wife, unborn baby.* Today. https://

www.today.com/news/widower-forges-
friendship-man-crash-killed-wife-unborn-
baby-2D12044681

Corporal Jason L. Dunham
    Congressional Medal of Honor Society. *Jason
    L Dunham | War on Terrorism (Iraq) | U.S.
    Marine Corps | Medal of Honor Recipient.*
    https://www.cmohs.org/recipients/jason-l-
    dunham Accessed 8 September 2025.

CHAPTER 3

Abortion
    Camosy, C. *Beyond the Abortion Wars.*
    https://www.charlescamosy.com/beyond-the-
    abortion-wars Accessed 9 September 2025.

Death penalty and prison reform

    Equal Justice Initiative. *Just Mercy.* https://
    justmercy.eji.org/ Accessed 9 September
    2025

    Stevenson, Bryan. *Just Mercy: A Story of
    Justice and Redemption.* Random House
    Publishing Group, 2015.

    Prejean, Helen. *Dead Man Walking: The
    Eyewitness Account of the Death Penalty That*

Sparked a National Debate. Knopf Doubleday
Publishing Group, 1994.

Malcolm X
National Museum of African American
History & Culture. *Who Was Malcolm X?*
https://nmaahc.si.edu/explore/stories/
malcolm-x Accessed 9 September 2025.

Marsha P. Johnson
National Women's History Museum. *Marsha
P. Johnson.* https://www.womenshistory.org/
education-resources/biographies/marsha-p-
johnson Accessed 9 September 2025.

CHAPTER 4

Anita Yellowhair
Alvarez, S. (2023, May 14). *No more silence:
Boarding school survivor Anita Yellowhair
shares her story, over 60 years later.* AZPM.
https://news.azpm.org/p/news-splash/
2023/5/14/215977-no-more-silence-
boarding-school-survivor-anita-yellowhair-
shares-her-story-over-60-years-later/

Indian Residential Schools

United States
Mejia, M. *The U.S. history of Native
American Boarding Schools.* The Indigenous

Foundation. https://www.theindigenous
foundation.org/articles/us-residential-
schools#:~:text=Approximately%20357
%20boarding%20schools
%20operated%20across%2030%20states,as
%20well%20as%20members%20of
%20the%20federal%20government Accessed
9 September 2025.

Canada
Rice, K. *Residential Schools and their Lasting
Impacts.* The Indigenous Foundation.
https://www.theindigenousfoundation.org/
articles/residential-schools-their-lasting-
impacts?rq=residential%20schools Accessed 9
September 2025.

Manosphere
Venkataramakrishnan, S. and Squirrell, T.
(2024, May 22). *The 'Manosphere'.* Institute
for Strategic Dialogue. https://
www.isdglobal.org/explainers/the-
manosphere-explainer/ Accessed 9 September
2025.

Boeing 737-MAX
Smiley, L. (2025, March 11). *The Worst 7
Years in Boeing's History—and the Man Who
Won't Stop Fighting for Answers.* Wired.
https://www.wired.com/story/boeing-
whistleblower-737-max/

Gerrymandering

Aguilar, R. and Razazan, M. (2025, August 15). *Trump-GOP gerrymandering scheme aims to rig the 2026 election.* KALW. https://www.kalw.org/show/your-call/2025-08-15/trump-gop-gerrymandering-scheme-aims-to-rig-the-2026-election

Fresh Air (2025, September 10). *The Future Of Free And Fair Elections.* NPR. https://www.npr.org/2025/09/10/nx-s1-5536996/the-future-of-free-and-fair-elections

Totenberg, N., et al. (2019, June 27). *Supreme Court Rules Partisan Gerrymandering Is Beyond The Reach Of Federal Courts.* NPR. https://www.npr.org/2019/06/27/731847977/supreme-court-rules-partisan-gerrymandering-is-beyond-the-reach-of-federal-court

2008 Financial Crash
Gratton, P. (2024, November 21). *Stock Market Crash of 2008: Explore the Causes and Events at the Heart of the Financial Crisis.* Investopedia. https://www.investopedia.com/articles/economics/09/subprime-market-2008.asp Accessed 10 September 2025

Criminalization of Homelessness
Ludden, J. (2024, June 28). *The Supreme Court says cities can punish people for sleeping in public places.* NPR. https://www.npr.org/2024/06/28/nx-s1-4992010/supreme-court-homeless-punish-sleeping-encampments

2025 Federal Budget Reconciliation
Chait, J. (2025, May 22). *The Largest Upward Transfer of Wealth in American History.* The Atlantic. https://www.theatlantic.com/ideas/archive/2025/05/big-beautiful-transfer-of-wealth/682885/

Synod on Synodality

Synod 2023. *Synod 2023 – Continental Assembly.* https://www.synod2023.org/ Accessed 20 September 2025.

White, C. (2021, October 10). *Pope Francis opens synod, encouraging church to master the 'art of encounter'.* NCR. https://www.ncronline.org/news/vatican/pope-francis-opens-synod-encouraging-church-master-art-encounter

Pope Francis

Brockhaus, H. (2020, April 8). *Pope Francis establishes new commission to study women*

deacons. Catholic News Agency. https://
www.catholicnewsagency.com/news/44137/
pope-francis-establishes-new-commission-to-
study-women-deacons

White, C. (2024, May 21). *Pope Francis
voices firm opposition to women deacons in
CBS interview.* National Catholic Reporter.
https://www.ncronline.org/vatican/vatican-
news/pope-francis-voices-firm-opposition-
women-deacons-cbs-interview

Big Oil & Gas

Disinformation campaign

McBean, G. (2024, May 29). *The oil and gas
industry has been lying about global warming
for decades—accountability is long overdue.*
The Conversation. https://
theconversation.com/the-oil-and-gas-
industry-has-been-lying-about-global-
warming-for-decades-accountability-is-long-
overdue-230160

Center for Climate Integrity. *How to identify
five lies the oil industry is still telling.* https://
climateintegrity.org/news/view/how-to-
identify-five-lies-the-oil-industry-is-still-
telling Accessed 9 September 2025.

House Committee on Oversight and
Accountability Democrats and Senate
Committee on the Budget. (2024, April).
*Denial, Disinformation, and Doublespeak: Big
Oil's Evolving Efforts to Avoid Accountability
for Climate Change.* https://www.budget.
senate.gov/imo/media/doc/fossil_fuel_
report1.pdf

Profits
Delouya, S. (2024 June 11). *Why oil
companies are raking in record profits under Joe
Biden.* CNN. https://www.cnn.com/
2024/06/11/economy/oil-industry-profits-
under-biden

Forever Chemicals
Aguilar, S. and Razazan, M. (2025,
September 8). *They Poisoned the World: The
Toxic History of Forever Chemicals.* KALW.
https://www.kalw.org/show/your-call/2025-
09-08/they-poisoned-the-world-the-toxic-
history-of-forever-chemicals

Food industry
Hyman, Mark. *The Blood Sugar Solution 10-
Day Detox Diet: Activate Your Body's Natural
Ability to Burn Fat and Lose Weight Fast.*
Little, Brown and Company, 2014.

The Trump Administration

Dismissed claims of voter fraud
Reuters. (2021, February 15). *Fact check: Courts have dismissed multiple lawsuits of alleged electoral fraud presented by Trump campaign.* Reuters. https://www.reuters.com/article/world/fact-check-courts-have-dismissed-multiple-lawsuits-of-alleged-electoral-fraud-p-idUSKBN2AF1FQ/

Dismantling of federal agencies

American Oversight. (2025, April 24). *The Trump Administration's Dismantling of Federal Agencies and Threats to Important Social Services.* https://americanoversight.org/investigation/the-trump-administrations-dismantling-of-federal-agencies-and-threats-to-important-social-services/ Accessed 9 September 2025.

American Oversight. (2025, February 25). *Trump's Illegal Firing of Inspectors General.* https://americanoversight.org/investigation/trumps-illegal-firing-of-inspectors-general/ Accessed 9 September 2025.

Reinstein, J. (2025, February 24). *Here are all the federal agencies where workers are being fired.* ABC News. https://abcnews.go.com/

US/agencies-federal-workers-fired/story?
id=118901289&utm

Berger, S. and Leibenluft, J. (2025, May 2).
*Trump Administration's Mass Layoffs of
Federal Workers Are Illegal.* Center on Budget
and Policy Priorities. https://www.cbpp.org/
research/federal-budget/trump-
administrations-mass-layoffs-of-federal-
workers-are-illegal Accessed 9 September
2025.

Razazan, M. and Aguilar, R. (2025, August
22). *Trump taps Project 2025 contributor to
lead the Bureau of Labor Stats.* KALW.
https://www.kalw.org/show/your-call/2025-
08-22/trump-taps-project-2025-contributor-
to-lead-the-bureau-of-labor-stats

Razazan, M. (2025, July 14). *Climate change,
federal budget cuts, and the Texas flooding
disaster.* KALW. https://www.kalw.org/show/
your-call/2025-07-14/climate-change-
federal-budget-cuts-and-the-texas-flooding-
disaster

Alana Chen
    Dear Alana, Official Website. https://
    dearalana.com/ Accessed 9 September 2025.

Russian aggression against Ukraine

Disinformation campaign
Stanley, J. (2022, February 26). *The antisemitism animating Putin's claim to 'denazify' Ukraine.* The Guardian. https://www.theguardian.com/world/2022/feb/25/vladimir-putin-ukraine-attack-antisemitism-denazify

Kidnapping of Ukrainian Children

Holligan, A. and Kuryshko, D. (2024, February 9). *Ukraine's missing children tracked down in Russia by digital sleuths.* BBC. https://www.bbc.com/news/world-europe-68249102

Cookman, L. (2025, September 16). *Russia has network of 200 camps for 'brainwashing' Ukrainian children – report.* The Guardian. https://www.theguardian.com/global-development/2025/sep/16/russia-has-network-of-200-camps-for-brainwashing-ukrainian-children-report

Ordination of women in the Catholic Church

Flannery, Austin, ed. *Vatican Council II: The Conciliar and Postconciliar Documents.* Liturgical Press, 2014.

Torjesen, Karen. *When Women Were Priests: Women's Leadership in the Early Church and the Scandal of Their Subordination in the Rise of Christianity.* HarperCollins, 1995.

Macy, Gary. *The Hidden History of Women's Ordination: Female Clergy in the Medieval West.* Oxford University Press, 2007.

O'Brien, John. *Women's Ordination in the Catholic Church.* Cascade Books, 2020.

Project: Ordination Justice
Father Anne Ministries. *Ordination Justice.* https://www.ordinationjustice.org/ Accessed 18 September 2025.

Gomes, J. (2025, June 12). *Zambian Sister Blows Whistle on 'Systemic' Clerical Sex Abuse of Nuns.* Bishop Accountability. https://www.bishop-accountability.org/2025/06/zambian-sister-blows-whistle-on-systemic-clerical-sex-abuse-of-nuns/

Associated Press. *India's hidden years of nuns sexually abused by priests.* (2019, January 2). Aljazeera. https://www.aljazeera.com/news/2019/1/2/indias-hidden-years-of-nuns-sexually-abused-by-priests

CHAPTER 5

Tatyana McFadden
MacKenzie, M. (2020, August 26). *Paralympic Champion Tatyana McFadden Is Smashing Stereotypes About Athletes With Disabilities.* Glamour. https://www.glamour.com/story/paralympic-champion-tatyana-mcfadden-is-smashing-stereotypes-about-athletes-with-disabilities

Nina Simone
Brandman, M. *Nina Simone.* National Women's History Museum. https://www.womenshistory.org/education-resources/biographies/nina-simone Accessed 10 September 2025.

Appalachia
Trista. (2025, July 22). *15 Harsh Truths About Growing Up Poor in Appalachian America.* History Collection. https://historycollection.com/15-harsh-truths-about-growing-up-poor-in-appalachian-america/

CHAPTER 6

Japanese internment
History.com Editors. (2025, May 28). *Japanese Internment Camps.* https://www.

history.com/articles/japanese-american-relocation Accessed on 10 September 2025.

Experimentation on enslaved women
  Holland, B. (2025, January 31). *The 'Father of Modern Gynecology' Performed Shocking Experiments on Enslaved Women.* History.com. https://www.history.com/articles/the-father-of-modern-gynecology-performed-shocking-experiments-on-slaves

History of slavery
  The New York Times. *The 1619 Project.* https://www.nytimes.com/interactive/2019/08/14/magazine/1619-america-slavery.html Accessed 20 September 2025.

Treatment of Indigenous Nations

  Dunbar-Ortiz, Roxanne. *An Indigenous Peoples' History of the United States (10th Anniversary Edition).* Beacon Press, 2023.

  DuVal, Kathleen. *Native Nations: A Millennium in North America.* Penguin Random House, 2025.

The Holocaust

  The National WWII Museum. (2024, May 8). *The Holocaust.* https://www.

nationalww2museum.org/war/articles/
holocaust Accessed September 10, 2025.

Stone, L. (2019, January 2). *Quantifying the Holocaust: Hyperintense kill rates during the Nazi genocide.* Science. https://www.science.org/doi/10.1126/sciadv.aau7292 Accessed 10 September 2025.

Chinese imprisonment of Uyghur people
Maizland, L. (2022, September 22). *China's Repression of Uyghurs in Xinjiang.* Council on Foreign Relations. https://www.cfr.org/backgrounder/china-xinjiang-uyghurs-muslims-repression-genocide-human-rights

Taliban's treatment of women
Hulst, R. and Onello, M. (2024, September 23). *Erased From Public Life: Women Under the Taliban Regime.* Ms. Magazine. https://msmagazine.com/2024/09/23/erased-from-public-life-women-under-the-taliban-regime/

U.S. Immigration and Customs Enforcement (ICE)

History of ICE
Abdelfatah, R., et al. (2025, September 4). *ICE.* NPR. https://www.npr.org/2025/09/04/nx-s1-5527309/ice

Inhumane conditions

Charalambous, P. and Romero, L. (2025, August 14). *'It's like you're dead alive': Families, advocates allege inhumane conditions at 'Alligator Alcatraz'.* ABC News. https://abcnews.go.com/US/youre-dead-alive-families-advocates-allege-inhumane-conditions/story?id=124645763

Dreisbach, T. (2023 August 16). *Government's own experts found 'barbaric' and 'negligent' conditions in ICE detention.* NPR. https://www.npr.org/2023/08/16/1190767610/ice-detention-immigration-government-inspectors-barbaric-negligent-conditions

Violence in Animal Research

PETA. *A Century of Suffering: 10 Gruesome Experiments on Animals From the Last 100 Years.* https://www.peta.org/features/history-of-animal-testing-10-shocking-experiments-last-100-years/ Accessed 10 September 2025.

Bekoff, M. and Goodall, Jane. (2025 March 24). *This is no way to treat humans' best friend.* The Washington Post. https://www.washingtonpost.com/opinions/2025/03/24/

dogs-experiments-cruel-ridglan-
prosecutor/?chead=true&

Colley, C. (2024, December 21). *US animal
lab from which monkeys escaped accused of
widespread abuse.* The Guardian. https://
www.theguardian.com/us-news/
2024/dec/21/animal-lab-monkeys-abuse-
allegations

Abuse of women under abortion bans

Associated Press (2022, June 10). *Salvadoran
women, jailed for decades for miscarriages,
stillbirths, warn the U.S. about abortion bans.*
NBC News. https://www.nbcnews.com/
news/latino/salvadoran-women-jailed-
decades-miscarriages-stillbirths-warn-us-
abort-rcna33035

Kekatos, M. (2025, June 19). *A pregnant
brain-dead woman in Georgia was kept on life
support. Experts say it raises ethical, legal
questions.* ABC News. https://
abcnews.go.com/Health/pregnant-brain-
dead-woman-georgia-life-support-
experts/story?id=122963319

Shaimaal-Sawaf
Shalash, F. (2024 March 6). *War on Gaza:
One woman mourns the loss of 50 family*

members in Israeli strikes. Middle East Eye.
https://www.middleeasteye.net/news/war-
gaza-50-family-members-loss

Israel-Gaza War

Hamas' October 7th attack on Israel

Kingsley, P., et al. (2023 December 22). *The
Day Hamas Came.* The New York Times.
https://www.nytimes.com/interactive/2023/
12/22/world/europe/beeri-massacre.html

Haroni, L., et. al. (2025, September 20).
*Hamas publishes archive photo of remaining 48
hostages, labeling them each as 'Ron Arad'.*
Yahoo News. https://www.yahoo.com/news/
articles/hamas-publishes-archive-photo-
remaining-140044844.html?
fr=sycsrp_catchall

Israeli attack on journalists
Aguilar, R. (2025 August 29). *Gaza is the
deadliest place on earth to be a journalist.*
KALW. https://www.kalw.org/show/your-
call/2025-08-29/gaza-is-the-deadliest-place-
on-earth-to-be-a-journalist

Famine in Gaza
World Health Organization. (2025 August
22). *Famine confirmed for first time in Gaza.*

https://www.who.int/news/item/22-08-2025-famine-confirmed-for-first-time-in-gaza Accessed 10 September 2025.

Destruction of Gaza

Garman, B., et al. (2025, July 18). *Israel levelling thousands of Gaza civilian buildings in controlled demolitions.* BBC. https://www.bbc.co.uk/news/resources/idt-33fccfbe-abcc-4af1-bdd2-632b2787cf59

Michie, I. and Benton, A. (2025, June 6). *All universities in Gaza have been destroyed. What does this mean for Palestinians?* ABC News. https://www.abc.net.au/news/2025-06-07/gaza-lost-generation-of-students-academic-say/105379150

Middle East Monitor. (2025 May 24). *At least 94% of hospitals in Gaza damaged or destroyed: UN.* https://www.middleeast monitor.com/20250524-at-least-94-of-hospitals-in-gaza-damaged-or-destroyed-un/ Accessed 10 September 2025.

CHAPTER 7

Malala Yousafzai
    The Nobel Prize. *Malala Yousafzai – Biographical.* https://www.nobelprize.org/

prizes/peace/2014/yousafzai/biographical/
Accessed 10 September 2025.

Dan Bigley
    Dan Bigley. *Grizzly Bear Attack Survivor.*
    http://danbigley.com/ Accessed 10
    September 2025.

Trump Administration's attack on DEI
    ACLU. (2024, July 2). *Trump on DEI And
    Anti-Discrimination Law.* https://
    www.aclu.org/trump-on-dei-and-anti-
    discrimination-law Accessed 14 September
    2025.

Nelson Mandela
    Nelson Mandela Foundation. *Biography of
    Nelson Mandela.* https://www.
    nelsonmandela.org/biography Accessed 10
    September 2025.

CHAPTER 8

Holocaust: Operation Reinhard
    Holocaust Encyclopedia. *Operation Reinhard.*
    https://encyclopedia.ushmm.org/content/en/
    article/operation-reinhard-einsatz-reinhard
    Accessed 10 September 2025.

Viktor Frankl
Frankl, Viktor E. *Man's Search for Meaning.*
Beacon Press, 2006.

Jewish revolt under the Roman Empire
PBS. *The Roman Empire: in the First Century.*
Enemies & Rebels. Josephus & Judea. https://
www.pbs.org/empires/romans/empire/
josephus.html Accessed 10 September 2025.

Crisis in Sudan
United Nations Regional Information Centre
for Western Europe (2025, September 1).
The UN and the crisis in Sudan. https://
unric.org/en/the-un-and-the-crisis-in-sudan-
jan-jun-2025/

Dorothy Day
Day, Dorothy. *The Long Loneliness: The*
Autobiography of the Legendary Catholic Social
Activist. Harper Collins, 2009.

The Catholic Worker Movement
The Catholic Worker Movement. *Catholic*
Worker Movement – A revolution of the heart.
https://catholicworker.org/ Accessed 10
September 2025.

Blues music
Pearley, L., Sr. (2018, May 9). *The Historical*
Roots of Blues Music. African American

Intellectual History Society. https://www.
aaihs.org/the-historical-roots-of-blues-music/

The Barefoot College
The Barefoot College. *The Real Barefoot
College.* https://barefoot.college/ Accessed 10
September 2025.

Restorative Justice for Oakland Youth
Restorative Justice for Oakland Youth.
RJOY – Restorative Justice for Oakland.
https://rjoyoakland.org/ Accessed 10
September 2025.

CHAPTER 9

Martin Luther King, Jr.
Stanford: The Martin Luther King, Jr.
Research and Education Institute. https://
kinginstitute.stanford.edu/ Accessed 10
September 2025.

The U.S. Civil Rights Movement
National Museum of African American
History & Culture. *Civil Rights History
Project.* https://nmaahc.si.edu/explore/
initiatives/civil-rights-history-project
Accessed 10 September 2025.

Civil Rights Act of 1964
> National Archives. *Civil Rights Act of 1964.*
> https://www.archives.gov/dc/highlights/civil-
> rights-act Accessed 10 September 2025.

Voting Rights Act of 1965
> National Archives. *Congress Protects the Right
> to Vote: The Voting Rights Act of 1965.*
> https://www.archives.gov/legislative/
> resources/education/voting-rights Accessed
> 10 September 2025.

Mendez, et. al v. Westminster school segregation
case
> Munemitsu, Janice. *About The Kindness of
> Color.* https://www.thekindnessofcolor.com/
> about/ Accessed 10 September 2025.

Supreme Court's gutting of the Voting Rights Act
of 1965

> Brennan Center for Justice. (2023, June 21).
> *Effects of Shelby County v. Holder on the
> Voting Rights Act.* https://www.brennan
> center.org/our-work/research-reports/effects-
> shelby-county-v-holder-voting-rights-act

> Singh, J. and Carter S. (2023, June 23).
> *States Have Added Nearly 100 Restrictive Laws
> Since SCOTUS Gutted the Voting Rights Act
> 10 Years Ago.* Brennan Center for Justice.

https://www.brennancenter.org/our-work/
analysis-opinion/states-have-added-nearly-
100-restrictive-laws-scotus-gutted-voting-
rights

Levy, P. (2025 August 5). *The Supreme Court
Prepares to End Voting Rights as We Know
Them.* Mother Jones. https://www.
motherjones.com/politics/2025/08/voting-
rights-act-supreme-court-2/

Genders in the Talmud
Scheinerman, R. *The Seven Genders in the
Talmud.* My Jewish Learning. https://www.
myjewishlearning.com/article/the-eight-
genders-in-the-talmud/ Accessed 10
September 2025.

Two-Spirit people
Thurston, I. *The History of Two-Spirit Folks.*
The Indigenous Foundation. https://www.
theindigenousfoundation.org/articles/the-
history-of-two-spirit-folks?rq=residential%20
schools Accessed 10 September 2025.

Intersex people
Intersex Campaign for Equality. *Promoting
human rights and equality for all intersex
people through art, education and action.*
https://www.intersexequality.com/ Accessed
10 September 2025.

Human Rights Watch. (2017 July 25). *US: Harmful Surgery on Intersex Children.* https://www.hrw.org/news/2017/07/25/us-harmful-surgery-intersex-children

Trans and nonbinary people
The Human Rights Campaign. *Transgender.* https://www.hrc.org/resources/transgender Accessed 10 September 2025.

Reed, Erin. *Erin In The Morning.* https://www.erininthemorning.com/ Accessed 10 September 2025.

Trans Legislation Tracker. *2025 anti-trans bills tracker.* https://translegislation.com/ Accessed 14 September 2025.

All the Only Ones. (2023, October 30). *NPR's new series All The Only Ones explores the lives of trans youth, past & present.* NPR. https://www.npr.org/about-npr/1208974806/npr-s-new-series-all-the-only-ones-explores-the-lives-of-trans-youth-past-presen

acknowledgments

To the small group of readers who sacrificed their time to read this manuscript and offer their excellent insights and encouragement; to my editors Jill and Kristen, who gave so generously of their incarnational gifts to make this manuscript shine brighter (any mistakes are mine alone); to my patrons who make my life as a Roman Catholic priest possible in the face of formidable institutional obstruction; to my advisors, who are always there when I need them; to the Society of Jesus and my brother Jesuits, who formed me into the priest I am today and whom I greatly miss since my excommunication; and especially, to God's Holy Spirit, to whom I am devoted, who never fails to guide me:

"I thank my God every time I remember you, constantly praying with joy in every one of my prayers for all of you because of your sharing in the gospel from the first day until now ."

—Philippians 1:3-5

+

an invitation to readers

Thank you for purchasing this book. Please recommend it to a friend. I survive on the support of people who want to build a better world. If you desire to learn more about how to pray or are interested in receiving spiritual direction to sort through the movements that surfaced during your engagement with this book, reach out to me at ordinationjustice@gmail.com. It is my privilege to accompany you on your journey of becoming in God.

Thank you for supporting ordination justice in the Roman Catholic Church.

+

about Father Anne

Father Anne was ordained on October 16, 2021 through a reform movement called the Association of Roman Catholic Women Priests. Because the Catholic Church excludes women from priesthood, Father Anne was forced by the institution to choose between obedience to God and obedience to Church law. Choosing God, she was excommunicated, ending her career in the Church she loves. She now devotes her life to the full participation of women in one of the most powerful institutions in the world. Father Anne has a Master of Divinity from Jesuit School of Theology and a Master of Arts in Rhetoric and Writing from San Diego State University. Her deepest desire is to serve as a parish priest in the Roman Catholic Church. She works for the day this dream comes true.

LEARN MORE:
www.fatheranne.com
www.ordinationjustice.org
www.shepherdwithin.com

+